PAPERCUTS
The Art of Self-Delusion

Brent Perkins

PAPERCUTS

The Art of Self-Delusion

www.3xBold.com

Copyright © 2023 Brent Perkins All Rights Reserved

No part of this publication may be reproduced, distributed, or transmitted in any form or by any means, including photocopying, recording, or other electronic or mechanical methods, without the prior written permission of the publisher, except in the case of brief quotations embodied in reviews and certain other non-commercial use permitted by copyright law.

Library of Congress Control Number: 2023913310

ISBN: 979-8-88759-986-1
ISBN: 979-8-88759-985-4
ISBN: 979-8-89109-110-8

PAPERCUTS

Outline

PREFACE	iv
CHAPTERS	
1 – Seasons	**2**
A Deep Thaw	4
The Cadence of Life	5
Winter Returns	14
Heat Induced	17
2 – Prepperations	**24**
Blissful Ignorance	25
Agency	30
Requiem	33
3 - Finding Reality	**38**
Absolutely Maybe	40
Fog of Illusion	46
Periscopes of Perception	53
Parallel Perspectives	58
Trustworthy	62
Final Framework	68
4 - Waking Up	**72**
Sleepwalking	72
A Special Gift	73
Distractions	77
Why Is Not the Question	82
A Shift	87
Conscious Decisions	93
The Power of Intent	98

5 - What's in the Mirror   **108**
    Reflections   108
    Corridor of Echoes   112
    Liar Liar   115
    Comfortably Fearful   121
    Wired This Way   126
    The Feels   133
    Projections   139

6 - Arching the Nemesis   **146**
    Sweet Stinger   149
    Anaphylaxis   155
    Deserving Better   160
    Similar Yet Different   167
    Fallacy-ism   174
    Land Mines   180
    Groundhogs   184
    Reflecting   192

7 - Learning To Fly   **196**
    Craftsmanship   196
    Dull Blades   203
    Tinnitus   221
    Inner Trust   217
    Just Show Up   224
    Meaningfully Specific   233

8 – Fluency   **242**
    Authentically Real   242
    Hide & Seek   248
    Chasing Happy   255

AFTERWORD   262

ACKNOWLEDGEMENTS   266

Dedication

This book was written for Brent Perkins (yes, myself).

If I am able to help myself, then I have done all that I can.
My deepest hope is that through my dedication to myself,
And the work that only I can do,
Somehow it touches others,
Inspiring them to look inside,
And do the work that only they can do.

PAPERCUTS

Preface

Hi, my name is Brent. I'm a Taurus. I like hiking, puppies, and....

Yuck!

We are not getting to know each other like this.
We are going to get vulnerable and go deep, quickly.

Let's try that again.

Hi, I'm Brent.

I'm a CEO and an entrepreneur. A dad. A friend. A lover (prioritized in that order).

I love my kids, my partner, my job, my friends, and all other life forms. I left God out for a reason. She's in there though, don't you worry.

I've underutilized many of my gifts.

I've manipulated and hurt a lot of people.

I messed up a marriage.

I didn't prioritize my kids in the way I wanted to.

I've disrespected my friends and other relationships.

I've lied. A lot. I mean, a lot, a lot.

I've been selfish.

I've been lazy.

I used drugs and alcohol to numb my pain and to hide behind.

I am my own worst critic and have treated myself like crap.

For most of my life, I never really liked myself, nor have I trusted myself.

This is who I've been, how I've thought, and the way I've shown up to life for the last 40 years. Today I have a few things to add to that list and the order, which matters immensely, gets a little readjusted. If it feels unclear as to why the order of things in these statements matters, I get it, and have addressed the significance of priorities in later chapters. The simplest explanation is that I have found that life requires us to choose, whether subconsciously or consciously, where we place our time and energy and, more importantly, where we don't.

Today, I can proudly say that:

I'm me (Brent), a dad, a brother, a friend, and a lover (in that order).

I love myself, my kids, and all other life forms (in that order).

I show up to life in the present moment.

I choose to be sober and clearheaded so I can experience and feel (and remember!) all of life.

I offer my superpowers of being bold, taking risks, entrepreneurship, creative writing, and deeply grounded presence as gifts to share with the world.

I love nature. It's my church. Hiking, biking, backpacking, skiing, you name it.

I love (playing) sports. Pickleball, tennis, basketball, beach volleyball.

I love myself—first and foremost, finally!

I trust myself.

I meditate and do breathwork to reconnect with myself and God—every day.

I practice mindfulness as often as my human brain allows.

I have a choice and I am creating daily.

I guess you could say that I have found a way to let love in. It hasn't been easy and the lessons along the way have sucked. Actually, they've been horrific at times. Perhaps I'm preaching to the choir here, and I am well aware that many of us have had 10x worse situations and experiences. It all hurts. It's all insanely difficult and exhausting at the soul level. Whatever it is that you've gone through or are going through, I won't diminish it. My heart sends you strength and peace. I have nothing but compassion for your journey.

This journey begins when we are willing to admit we have lost control. We have relinquished our power and are no longer in the driver's seat, making decisions and owning our choices. Maybe we're in deferral mode, allowing our reptilian brain to run amuck while we live in constant fear. Our minds are in a heightened state of alert and are filled with chemicals designed to save our life, not run our day. This eventually leads to a shutdown, as the subconscious chooses for us.

This is the "when" and "where" of how we get stuck in life. When we aren't creating, stepping into our inner artist, owning our power of choice and expressing it to the world, we open ourselves up and are vulnerable to getting hurt. Usually by hurting ourselves. Whether that be our own inner critic or the external noise we allow past our filters, ultimately polluting our fragile self-image. The result is that mental health, specifically anxiety and depression, has become the most prolific disease we are faced with as a society today.

A vast majority is also not pathological. It's learned, which means it's preventable and can be unwound. Learning how to take ownership of and control over our innate ability to effect the changes we so desire is part of our birthright and possibly the only way to put an end to the pain and suffering our blindness has on ourselves, our families, and on society. The solution is simple, though not easy. It's free yet requires the deepest level of commitment. And there is no waiting, as we have access to the answer right now.

Papercuts: The Art of Self-Delusion attempts to address the global lack of self-awareness around the power we each have over our individual experiences, the depth of agency over all aspects of life, and the impact our interpretations of those experiences have on our psyche.

Generational trauma, though not directly addressed in the following pages, cannot be ignored. It deserves a center stage acknowledgment and an intense focus. Until then, the lessons in this book offer the tools necessary to build a strong foundation, allowing you to step into that space, with both feet, when the time is right in your life.

If you still aren't sure if this book is for you, that's okay. As I already told you, this book is for me. That's why I wrote it. Or God wrote it. I honestly don't know who wrote it. It did come through my fingers, though.

If one of the following resonates with you, your time spent here will not be wasted.

- You've hit a wall. Feel blocked. Stumped. Like you're at an impasse.
- The women, who, to reach their goals and dreams, have had to adopt masculine behaviors, especially in the workforce.
- The men who've felt obligated to provide and be the breadwinners, at all costs.
- You have been bullied and had your self-esteem trampled on.
- You have lived through abuse, be it physical or psychological.

- You feel the need or desire to prove to your parents, friends, or the world you could do it. That you are good enough.

- You're part of the "I'm already happy" or "life is mostly good" crowd.

- You. As you are. Just you.

However, and whoever you are, there is a nugget of wisdom here that you need, which is why you found this book, or it found you.

I'd be honored to be your guide on this journey. To walk shoulder to shoulder as things unfold in the chapters ahead. The entry fee is honesty, vulnerability, and a little GAS. When we Give-A-Shit (GAS) about ourselves, our friends, and our family then we have access to curiosity. Being curious allows us to set aside skepticism, pessimism, and a lack of desire to embrace change. In my life, I've adopted the "could be good, could be bad, who knows" mentality as I lean into curiosity and let new adventures unfold.

Whether you're all in or still have a little trepidation, let's kick this off with an intent that will unify our time together. Feel free to modify the intent and make it your own or you can read the following out loud with me.

INTENT: *"I desire to be present, for myself first and foremost, and to hear, maybe for the first time, the inner voice, the guide, or spirit that lives inside of me. The one who always has my best interest at heart and is here to protect me, even when that safety comes with a lesson of pain and heartache. I commit to only picking this book up and consuming the stories and rituals inside of it after I get myself calm, centered, and have shaken off the distractions of the day. I do all of this in honor of myself, because I deserve it."*

The following is my story. Most of it is from the perspective of the voice in the head. Which means it's *only* my story. If you know me and your version is slightly different, then that's perfect. It's how it should be (you'll find out more as to why a little later in the book).

That's it. Let's get this show on the road!

*One last thing. You will find virtually no reference to male and female pronouns, with a small exception. Throughout the following conversation, the ego is referred to as "he" and the higher Self is referred to as "She." God or spirit may also be referred to as "She."

Why? Our society most commonly associates the masculine with traits like assertiveness, competitiveness, being grounded, and rational, which are traits of the ego, or the individual self. On the other hand, the feminine has been linked to qualities like nurturing, empathy, creativity, and intuition, which are traits of the higher self, or the transcendent, spiritual part of the self.

Neither of these associations have anything to do with gender, including any social or cultural meanings and expectations associated with being male, female, or any other identifications.

PAPERCUTS

Chapter 1:
SEASONS

"Wake the fuck up!"

My eyes flashed open. The breath sucked right out of me. I knew that voice. *Where was I?*

Damn! That was the most vivid and realistic dream I've ever had. Bordered by soaring cliffs on both sides, I found myself at the helm of our raft, crushing a level 4 rapid. Barely avoiding an eddy as we slammed sideways into a protruding boulder, our boat nearly tipping. Water rushing in as it slammed us all down against the hard deck. The desert heat typical of the Grand Canyon finding itself evasive at the tail end of the fall season.

If only. It turns out that sixteen ounces of ice water thrown at your face will wake anyone from even the deepest of slumbers.

I bolted up, instantly pulled into the realm of the living. My eyes unable to stay open as the overnight goo that had built up along the edges pulled the skin of the lids back down. Breathing was difficult, a rapid yet shallow cycle. My mind, aimlessly scanning all five senses, trying with all the presence I could muster to make sense of the situation.

The light from the hallway cast a shadow across the bed and over my face. It all seemed surreal, making it that much harder to gain footing on what in the heck was happening. The remnants of the bottle of wine from four hours earlier still swirled through my head, preventing me from getting a grip on reality. The whole situation felt slippery, mentally and physically, as water dripped from my hair, down my cheeks, and onto my legs.

I recoiled as my eardrums sent signals in every direction at lightning speed. It felt like a shot had been fired across my proverbial bow. My breath grew ragged at the sight of my wife hovering in the doorway, though I could only make out her silhouette. She was at the end of her rope and lacked the tools necessary to express herself in any other way. Her emotions erupted all over the place, like a volcano, spitting its lava straight at my face. Smoke billowed out and thickened the air, paralyzing everything in its path. Words started to form in my head, but got stuck there. The normal path to my tongue and vocal cords was blocked. Paralysis had its grip on my entire body.

Blinking, breathing, blinking, breathing. I tapped all the strength I could find as my hand finally obeyed the command I had been shouting for the last few minutes. Feeling the depth of wetness that my hair held and wiping it down my face, things started to come into focus.

"*Wake the fuck up!*" the gray shadow in the doorway bellowed a second time.

It reverberated through the dense air that filled the room. Over and over again, the same four words are all I can remember hearing. The realization set in that my shirt, shorts, and the bed around me were all soaked, and I started to shiver. It was summer in Phoenix, lending the 70-degree air-conditioned house to be less than friendly to a water-soaked zombie at three in the morning.

I don't remember what happened from here. Between the shock of the water, the ear-piercing lecture, the alcohol haze, and the liquid fear pulsing through my veins, I have no recollection of any further details. At least not from the middle of that night. It would be amazing if I could sit here and tell you that this was my wake-up call. That this was how I became aware of my transgressions, and it started me down a path to enlightenment and positive changes in my life.

This was in early 2020. The truth would prove to be much more elusive.

--- -- - *A Deep Thaw* - -- ---

The journey I am currently on officially started about 12 years before the 3 am water wake-up drill. In 2008, at the age of thirty, an alarm went off in my soul. I can't put my finger on the exact moment it happened, but I started to question things in life, the world around me, the Christian religion I was indoctrinated into at such a young age, my friends, and what was universally (or just my mom's viewpoint) "good and bad" or "right and wrong." Was there even such a thing? None of it made sense. None of it was how I was promised it would be. My core beliefs were all lies, or so they felt. This *reality* I was living in, setting goals for and working my ass off in, was a house of cards. It was fake. Pure bullshit. Built on the fears of society. The norms and expectations of all those around me. The list of "shoulds" on my plate was stacked to the ceiling and wobbling in an ever-widening circumference.

The early days of my journey took me into the study of ancient cultures, their religions, spirituality, and fascination with the cosmos. Reading about the 25,000-year-old cave paintings, 12,000-year-old ceremonial sites, and the unfathomably similar architecture that dotted the globe sparked my own desire to see these sights firsthand. Fast-forward five years and I find myself lying in the supposed sarcophagus of Khufu, inside the King's chamber of the Great Pyramid. An ancient energy, one that holds the key needed to decipher the stories of an older epoch, engulfed me. The guide I was with had me sit across from him while he hummed. The entire chamber started vibrating and my body became a tuning fork, buzzing in coherence with the reverberating frequencies. To this day, the experience leaves me shaking my head in awe and utterly speechless.

Around the world there are hundreds of ancient sites, built with megaliths, that we still can't make sense of today.

Whether how to build and construct them or why these early cultures would spend their time and energy on such things when food, water, shelter, and sex should have been their only focus. The incongruences I kept uncovering coalesced and formed a backstory that lay in complete contrast to my understanding of history. Virtually none of these cultures and the validity of their stories are supported by modern religions, yet they can't be ignored.

I could no longer sit back and take the lessons and explanations that filled my childhood at face value. "Don't worry, Brent, nice guys always win in the end," my mom would say, or "Jesus loves you and that's all that matters." One of my favorites was, "Native Americans are going to hell unless they choose to believe in Jesus." And what about the indigenous cultures that existed without the knowledge of Jesus? Somehow, my mom and the church had all the answers, and we were just supposed to blindly follow the wisdom of scholars much more spiritual and connected than I was led to believe that I would ever be.

For me, the church had ruled my life since I was a toddler. The music I was allowed to listen to, the type of people I hung out with, my language, my food and drink, my weekend activities, dating and interaction with the opposite sex, morality at large. The religious Kool-Aid I grew up on condemned and judged the world in a way that I knew, or maybe hoped that someday would be proved, couldn't be universally true. The more I read and visited these sacred locations around the globe, the angrier I got. How could I have been so deceived? Everything I believed was false or, at the very least, needed a new perspective and narrative. The more I questioned, the more the guilt and shame tactics used on me throughout my youth resurfaced and went to work on me again.

Being in my early 30s at the time, this was truly soul-rattling. Questioning the foundation that my entire life had been built upon was confusing. Frustrating. Mind-boggling. And I took it out on the world around me. My disdain for other people grew to a point of excess, one that was downright unhealthy. So much so that, even in my blinding anger, I saw the wall of self-righteousness my ego was building around me. Stacking itself higher and higher. Brick by brick. Leaving room for a moat of sarcasm as a secondary defense. Both specifically designed to protect my inner sanctum. I no longer cared how it hurt me or all the others who lied to me and caused me to be in this place of starting over. I trusted no one, especially not myself. How could I be wrong and not know it for so long?

--- -- - *The Cadence of Life* - -- ---

Ignoring what was right in front of me, most likely because of the pain it brought, I shifted focus. Compartmentalizing the ugly parts, I spent the next decade chasing my career goals, much of which was influenced by the aspirations and lofty goals I had set for myself at a very young age. My dad was an entrepreneur who started multiple companies and then retired in his early fifties. That's not how it was supposed to go though. At least not in my pipedream where his retirement would signal a ceremonial passing of the baton in the semi-family business he was running.

I had worked my way up through his company, doing the absolute bottom-end grunt work, just to prove my resilience and willingness to do any and everything it took to be the best. To be ready and able, sidestepping any projected nepotism. It sounds like I'm minimizing the effort here, but from the age of twelve, I took painstakingly specific steps to make sure I wouldn't fail or be told I did it wrong. That wasn't going to happen on my watch.

During my college years, things became less stable for my dad. As his company saw more success, the challenges grew as well. His tenure ended in an accusation, albeit unfounded and ultimately relinquished, of sexual misconduct. The writing was on the wall, and he chose to bow out of his role and sell his shares. That was right at the end of my college stint. With my hopes and dreams dashed, I had to scramble to figure out what I was going to do in the real world.

They say the apple doesn't fall far from the tree and that held true for me. I found myself, at the end of my twenties, having started two businesses and currently jobless, trying to pick up the pieces after the financial crisis of 2008. Married and with two daughters in tow, I felt the pressure of the world on my shoulders to perform and provide. It took two years to find my way back to the game, but when I did, it was a full-court press. In three years' time I worked my way through the ranks of a small biotech company to become CEO. I had made it! All my dreams had come true.

Look at me! That's right, society. I did it. Goal achieved.

Now that I was a CEO, I let it set its hooks deep into me. I let it consume me, take over my life, and define who and what I was. The doors it opened, the other executives I surrounded myself with, the events I got invited to, the pomp and ceremony of all those around me, sucked in by the other lonely CEOs, constantly finding ways to celebrate our awesomeness and hold on to that feeling of importance. It was like a support group whose mission was to constantly remind ourselves that we were extra special. If we didn't tell ourselves how special we were, who was going to?

I don't know whether it was the role, society's expectations, or the lies I told myself, but I made everything else in my life play second fiddle to my career. I paid virtually no attention to myself and my health or fitness needs. My marriage suffered as I ignored and relegated my partner to second position. My kids got the bare minimum. Between the 100 days a year I was traveling around the globe and the other 100 late nights, I was unable to find the energy or time to be present with any of my family.

It's alright though, because I was doing all of this for them after all.

This was my narrative. It was what allowed me to get a good night's sleep, and it was one of the biggest lies I told myself and my family. It was a convenient story, which made me feel justified and good. Whole even. I mean, how can such a selfless act and sacrifice be questioned?

Somewhere along the way, the emptiness of this existence started to set in. I felt a tug. It was beckoning me to something else. Somewhere else. I knew there was more. More than I was currently ignoring or numbing away. My research into ancient cultures, the prehistory of man, and religions of antiquity all pointed to the grand scale of our existence. The same one that I had been living in, yet at the ignorant level of a myopic human only concerned about today and, maybe, tomorrow.

Unable or unwilling to see beyond the bubble that present day society had me caught in, I needed a break. Time to collect my thoughts and figure out what my next move was. So, I did what any other successful executive would do and booked a three-day trip to Hawaii with plans to wallow in my confusion and pain, all while numbing myself (mostly with alcohol). Ah, paradise!

Twenty minutes before boarding, they called my name to the kiosk. As I walked up and confirmed my name, the lady behind the counter handed me a new ticket. "You've been upgraded," she said dryly. Sweet! All those miles traveled did pay off from time to time. As I boarded the plane, all I could think about was ordering a glass of wine, shutting my brain down, and escaping the web of shit I had spun my life around.

Being first to board a plane has its advantages. I didn't have to struggle with finding space for my carry-on or wait in line as everyone located their seat and struggled to tuck themselves into the small claustrophobic space that they paid hundreds of dollars for the luxury of being confined to for the next five hours. Finding my seat, I closed the window shade, opened my book, and tried to drown out the commotion encircling me like buzzards who smelled fresh roadkill on a hot Arizona afternoon.

"Hey," came a friendly voice along with a whoosh of air as she plopped into the seat next to me. "Hey back at you," I said, smiling, then quickly went back to whatever book I was reading at the moment. She wasn't having that, though. Apparently, we were going to talk. A lot.

Whatever details I might fill in next are splotchy at best. What I do know is that the woman next to me was intriguing. Pretty without trying. Smart, witty, funny, and a little off. In the best way possible. She got me to put my book down and start talking. About what, I can't quite remember. I do know that our flight got delayed due to mechanical issues.

As we sat there chatting away, waiting for the plane to be fixed, she pulled out a deck of Tarot cards. "Can I read these for you," she said with an impish grin. "Ha, sure," I snorted. And that was the beginning of my newfound friendship and lifelong path to self-awareness.

We deplaned. Hung out in the terminal together. Got on a new plane. Spent the next five hours talking. Being vulnerable. Going deep. It turned out that she was an author who had just recently finished her first book, *Expectation Hangover*. Her name was Christine Hassler (she is now married to her king, an incredible dude who I fully approve of—not that she asked). After we got off the plane, I gave her a ride to her hotel, and we exchanged emails. What a whirlwind. And I never did get that glass of wine or even bother to think about it. My mind was spinning in circles.

Christine and I spent the next nine months working together. We did the virtual thing way before that was mainstream. It worked though, and she became the catalyst for the new direction of my lifelong journey. No one had ever held space for me like that before. I'm not sure if she knows, even to this day, what a special gift this was for me.

Life, and my understanding of it, started to shift in a positive direction for me internally, yet externally it grew worse. I questioned things even deeper and doubted myself more. Time spent on me became top priority, the only priority at times. I struggled with the concept of balance. I still do. It's a daily battle that requires effort and presence. Oh, and grace. Lots of grace.

During a monthly event at one of the mastermind groups I was part of, I met another amazing woman, Vered Kogan, founder of the Momentum Institute and the MINDset Game podcast. I was blown away at the intellectual understanding around softer, more woo-woo topics of the heart and head that Vered had. She introduced me to the connection that breathing, heart coherence, and our brains have to each other. As someone who gets stuck in their head way too often and innately relies on intellect over intuition, the correlation and connection she helped me to understand was game-changing.

I could see the light at the end of the tunnel, possibly for the first time.

It became vividly clear I wasn't happy, satisfied, or on my life path anymore when it came to my job. Within six months I found myself typing my resignation and breaking up with the Board of Directors, who were 5,000 miles away in Finland. I hadn't been happy for about two years, and I was in search of something that better aligned with where I was currently at on my journey. Very quickly I found a new company that needed a CEO with my skill set. Same title. Different industry. Different ownership group. Different means better, right? Yeah, not exactly.

It took almost three years to integrate the initial lessons Christine and I worked on. The process felt like stirring a cold jar of molasses that had just been taken out of the fridge. With the recent change in careers and all the work I was putting into leveling up, the lessons started to get traction at a much faster pace. Things were warming up and the forward progress was getting easier and more fluent. I could finally step into the driver's seat of my life, making at least some conscious choices instead of letting them all default to my automatic cyclical patterns.

By spring of 2019, including some of the stuff Vered and I worked on, most lessons were getting sticky after 3–6 months of conscious work on them. For anyone who knows me well, patience is not one of my virtues. I like to see change immediately and these lessons were happening and integrating way too slow for my liking. I felt amazing and terrible all at the same time. And through it all, nothing changed with my marriage, my kids, or, frankly, my love for myself. While I had opened to new perceptions of life, nothing landed in the way I hoped for.

--- -- - *Winter Returns* - -- ---

Splash.

Shaking off the confusion and spraying water everywhere, I sprung out of bed and slipped on the floor. Not wanting more icy water thrown on me, I lunged to shut and lock the guest bedroom door. Back to that early morning in 2020, I found myself floating above my body, watching it squirm and shiver. I had to laugh at how silly my earthly body looked, straining to figure out what the next move was. My head was pounding. My thoughts were murky. I needed sleep. So, I shut out the world, turned off my brain, and wrapped myself in a moist cocoon of wet blankets.

I don't know whether I dislike being cold, wet, or just the word "moist" the most. Either way, the next four hours were miserable. When I finally woke up, that was when I knew.

My marriage was over, it had been for years.

My way of life had to change. Living a life of integrity was no longer an option.

My approach to business and who I believed I had been was about to be reprogrammed.

What I used to see as evil, I finally saw for what it really is: fear and pain. Most shockingly, I learned that the fear and pain around me were mostly mine. Whenever it looked external to myself, and I wanted to play the victim card, it was always the projection of my fears. 100% of the time.

"Damn," I pondered, "This is going to be a lot of hard work."

Even after resentment had turned into contempt, it took another two years, more missteps, more pain, more suffering, and more lack of self-love before my marriage officially ended. I certainly didn't hold up my end of the bargain. I projected onto everyone in my family. I tried to control my inner world by controlling them along with my outer world.

I disrespected myself, which meant I automatically disrespected my family. The two go hand in hand. I know that now. You can't give what you don't have.

The 18 months after we separated were the most life-changing for me. Don't get me wrong, the first 60 days were bottom-of-the-barrel horrific. Everything was turned upside down, inside out and stability was nowhere in sight. I quickly realized that this was going to get ugly if I continued to enable the downward spiral. And I probably would have if I didn't have two daughters who needed a dad. That's not to say that I didn't royally screw up and model awful behavior along the way. I did. Call it the grace of God, divine intervention, my guardian angel, the holy spirit, or my dead Uncle Jim working out a piece of his own karma while in Purgatory, but it was like someone perfectly placed a trampoline under me to break my fall. I was able to springboard myself out of the muck and back onto the path I had worked so hard on over the last 10+ years.

In the end, unconditional love, for myself and others, has been the biggest lesson. As a society, we have conditions for everything, and we're darn good at justifying them too. Finding authentic unconditional love for myself has set the stage in such a different way. I now trust myself, which means self-doubt is gone (mostly—I am still human, after all), and doing things to make other people happy, at my expense, is a thing of the past and always a "hell no."

I understand that my health, wealth, and happiness are the most important things in the world, and the words selfish and narcissistic are only implied or projected purely out of jealousy. Knowing that we can't give what we don't have, I live under the mandate that we must give to ourselves first and foremost.

So, yes, I've been all these things and none of them. I have chosen to embrace and relish change. To choose differently. To choose me, which, oddly enough, brings the grandest impact to everyone else in my life.

"The best gift you can give to those you love is to become the best version of yourself." Thank you, Tony! And that, Mr. Robbins, takes effort. It means going deep and doing the work.

Circling back to a judgment I made about Christine earlier in my journey makes me giggle. Just like my initial judgment of her, I, too, now consider myself just a bit "off."

And I'm damn proud of it!

--- -- - *Heat Induced* - -- ---

The story of my journey, to date, pays homage to a part of me I no longer let run rampant. The inner monologue. The never-ending voice that analyzes the past and foretells the future. The one that prevents all of us from being in the present. The part that dreams up elaborate expectations, which is why our society has concocted so many techniques and tools, mostly unhealthy, to quiet this voice. To offer us a moment's reprieve.

It's this part of our inner self that we're going to take a look at together. Whether we have to sweet talk our way there or use our machete to carve out a new path, we will find our way to a place where it no longer controls us or negatively serves us.

If you're like me and enjoy Thai food, there's a good chance the word alone evokes happy memories of the aromas, tastes, and lingering spices that tickle the tongue after a first bite. I can live this fantasy through Mexican, Ethiopian, Indian, and countless other cuisines. The level of heat available in these styles of cooking is rarely enjoyed or appreciated when we are kids, though. In fact, any level of spice heat is arguably horrific and traumatic.

I can remember, on more than one occasion, taking a bite, my eyes widening and bugging out, the alarm going off in my head, with my legs bolting for the sink, trying not to spit the food out on the way. Half a gallon of milk later, with the inflammation in the back of my throat slowly subsiding and finally being able to muster my wits, I choked out, "This is insane. Who can eat food like this?" Still panting and bent at the waist with hands on my knees, it seemed like an eternity before the pain subsided.

Tears formed and, at one point, streamed down my face. The well was dry now and I wiped the remnants from my cheeks. Bringing the room into focus, I could see my parents trying to maintain their composure. Lips pressed in concern, but their eyes ratted them out. That squinted smile that only the outside creases of the eyes can contort into. It made my blood boil. What in the heck was possibly so funny about this situation?

Of course, they were concerned, but at 13 years old, they knew I was in no real danger. While I vowed to never understand why adults like spicy things, it did open my mind to various possibilities. The prospect of the unknown and that change were real and alive. Keeping an open and curious mind, I wondered who and what I would become. To this day, staying curious has been one of the attributes that has served me best in life.

It's probably no surprise that I love spicy food today. For a couple of years, I put hot sauce or red pepper flakes on virtually everything I ate. I couldn't get enough of the undulating waves of sensation that flowed from my mouth, up through my nose, and out through my extremities. That burn. The sweat that followed it. Then a whole-body tingling that is quite exhilarating and addicting! I only craved the next fix from whatever ranked high enough on the Scoville scale. Food itself became an afterthought, nothing more than the delivery vehicle for the hot divinity that lit my mouth up and sent my eyes rolling to the back of my head. And I almost always ordered my Thai food at a Level 5 out of 5. Give it to me hot!

At some point it dawned on me that I didn't know what food tasted like anymore. My senses were dulled by the obsessive amounts of spice I increasingly required. Apples no longer tasted good. Bananas were bland. Steak lost all the mineral tang that makes it so unique. It was time for a break. Change was in order.

It took about two weeks of cutting out all heat or warming spices from my diet before I felt a shift. It was 6:25 am on a Tuesday when it smacked me in the face. Literally. I had just finished cutting up a mango for my daughter's breakfast and stabbed a chunk with my fork, making sure it was ripe and would be how she enjoyed it. That first bite was like an explosion in my mouth. Could it be that this was the best mango I had ever had? Doubtful.

An unopened package of yellow snacking tomatoes stared at me from across the kitchen, nestled right next to my coffee machine. I ripped the top layer of cellophane off and popped one in my mouth. Seeds and juice sprayed the back of my tongue as I bit down. The acidic sweetness caused me to take a deep breath through my nose. Wow. Just wow! Next, I grabbed a strawberry popsicle out of the freezer. An all-fruit one with real sugar of the organic kind. Tearing off the wrapper, I bit off a chunk, chewed it once, and pressed the icy slush against the roof of my mouth. Bolts of flavor shot down the sides of my mouth. I closed my eyes and shook my head. Damn! Where has this been my whole life? My mouth was dancing with delight.

I have since reintroduced spicy elements into my diet, but with conscious design. There are days when it's in my salad for lunch but not my dinner. There might be a jalapeño in my omelet and nothing else spicy for the rest of the day. I may occasionally do a five-day spice fast. The point is, I mix it up. Spice is no longer necessary for me to enjoy food. In fact, it's a detriment at times.

We rarely need a Level 5 in our life. I say "rarely" as I am well aware that a Level 5 can be a lot of fun and, conversely, is needed from time to time to kick us in the butt. That's what it took for me to learn the painful lessons that kept smacking me across the face for all those years.

To finally wake up, pay attention, and start showing up for life.

Here's to the spice of life. May it guide us well (and hold our hand when we need it) on this journey together.

PAPERCUTS

Chapter 2:
PREPPERATIONS

The buzzer was ringing. Silence fell over the crowd. You could hear the in-breath of every soul in the bleachers as the ball arced and rotated toward the hoop.

Whoosh.

The sweetest sound in basketball. Three points for our team! And that was a wrap for my daughter's high school basketball team. At least for the regular season. That final three-pointer broke the tie and secured her team's place in the upcoming state playoffs.

Another week would pass before the teams got re-seated and who was playing against who got announced. As expected, an email was sent around the following Friday, full of excitement and to-dos. Our team was headed to Flagstaff, Arizona, as one of the high schools there was ranked 5th to our 12th seat, so they were the hosting school. I felt a pinch, a tickle, a tap. Almost like the feeling of a small twig snapping under foot while walking in the woods.

Oh, yeah. Duh. This was the same high school that one of my oldest friends had gone to. *"Gosh, we haven't talked in what seems like ages,"* I thought to myself. It had been almost two years since we had last seen each other. And I was fairly certain he lived within a few miles of there. That was the nudge from the universe that I needed to reach out to him.

--- -- - *Blissful Ignorance* - -- ---

The following week I pulled into his circular driveway, stepped out into the mid-afternoon sun, and was greeted by his daughter. High fives were in order, as she didn't remember me well enough to give hugs. I stepped into the madness of what planning headquarters looks like the day before a 300-person charity dinner. It was a coordinated hustle. Bodies danced and fluttered about, making the most of the burning daylight. This wasn't his day job, but a passion project he spearheads every year as his way to give back to the community.

"Hey, my man!" My friend stepped out from behind a stack of boxes, full of donations for the charity auction. We embraced in a hug that only old friends who know way too much about each other can do. Our friendship goes back to our second year of college, so we've seen it all together.

He wrapped things up and gave some final directions to his staff before we headed off for an early dinner. By the time we got seated, there was barely an hour before I needed to leave for the basketball game. We were going to need more time.

I let him ask most of the questions. On the surface, it appeared that more had changed in my life than his over the last couple of years. While this probably wasn't reality, we didn't have much choice with our limited time. He went through the family questions, the job, my divorce, health, fitness, and romantic relationships. All the normal stuff.

Then we got to this book. I went through my normal spiel about how I felt called to write this book. To quit my job and share this story in an effort to bring awareness to those who are stuck yet also seeking answers. Addressing the contingent among us that knows there is more to life, relationships, and the universe as a whole. That the lack of self-love is leading to the lack of self-care, which is contributing to a lot of pain, depression, and anxiety in our world.

He sat cockeyed in his chair, listened intently, respectfully, and took a long breath before responding. *"Brent,"* he said through a long exhale. *"I don't know what life is like for you, but we think differently here. We're in a small town. We enjoy nice things but in a much simpler way. I love my life. I love my wife, my kids, and my career. We party, but not too hard. We play but with balance. We work hard and are proud of it."*

I didn't know what to say. My story, the one you just read about, has resonated and landed with almost everyone I know. And here was one of my oldest friends, either not really hearing me or telling me that I missed the mark somehow. Once the confusion and fear washed over me, I quickly came back to the present and reset myself.

Instead of pushing or selling him on my why, I shared another story with him about my truth. One that led to me realizing that I hadn't shown up for my family, my friends, or myself over the years. The impact it's had on them and me, simultaneously, and how I have worked hard to show up differently today. The appreciation I hold for the opportunity to have seen these missteps and a chance to move forward with different intentionality.

There was something about the vulnerability of this story that caused him to move past it. Sitting up straight in his chair, he paused to look down. With a soft leveling of his gaze, he said, *"As your friend, I will, of course, read your book. But I don't want to."*

"Oh?" I said, perplexed.

Looking me dead in the eye, he said:

"What if I don't want to know?
What if I don't want to find out?
That I'm an alcoholic.
An asshole.
A narcissist."

(Oh, shit)

"*I get it*," was all I could think to say in the moment.

And I meant it.

While I hadn't considered his position before, it made total sense. It hit me right in the chest. Hard, too. How could I have overlooked and been blind to his vantage point? His disclosure was so real and honest.

I sent him the following message when I got home the next day:

"It was really good to see you today. Thank you for the conversation, our friendship, and dinner. You have a beautiful family, an amazing home, and I can see why you are so comfortable with the life you've worked so hard to build. I am so happy for you!"

The more I thought about it, the more friends, colleagues, and acquaintances came to mind that fall into this same category of thought. Those that believe life is good. Fun. Satisfying. The love in my life is real. It's conditional at times, but it's *real*. My relationships are good. My family is good. My income is good. I'm healthy. Maybe it's not ultimately fulfilling at the soul level, but who has that really?

Why screw up a good thing?

In 2003, when he was at the top of his game, Tiger Woods made a decision that shocked the world. He had remarkable success utilizing the same swing style for many years. But he was also conscious of the fact that golf was continuously changing, and he realized that to remain the best in the world, he would need to modify his strategy. He wanted to improve even more, and he thought that altering his swing would enable him to do so.

Such a monumental endeavor was not an easy choice for him, and Tiger understood that learning a new skill would be difficult and, indeed, a lot of effort. He was also aware that altering his swing might have a short-term negative impact on his performance and cause him to lose some, if not most, of his competitive edge. The whole experiment also ran the risk of backfiring completely, preventing him from ever being the best again, not to mention the millions, possibly hundreds of millions, of dollars at stake.

This had to be the scariest and most difficult thing Tiger had ever decided to do, and it took an immense amount of courage. The next two years were filled with a lot of heartache, setbacks, and frustrations. His perseverance paid off in the end, though, resulting in one of the most prestigious and coveted of his wins at the 2005 Masters tournament.

Change is risky. It requires stepping into the unknown. The daydream of possibility.

--- -- - *Agency* - -- ---

If I have learned anything during the course of my life and while writing this book, it's that we get to decide what, if anything, we might get out of our time here on Earth. Whether you choose to deny or go as far as embracing our most powerful and underutilized gift, the path we are walking is one of rediscovering our free will, and how we're wasting it. Life is about choice, at every juncture. Every second, really. Even choices we make unconsciously, for the most part, are a choice.

Quite simply, this book is about choice.

Only it's not. As simple as making choices may seem, it's been the hardest lesson I've had to learn in my life. Isn't it funny how the simple things are sometimes the most complicated?

Thanks a lot, God!

No, seriously, thank you for giving us something so powerful yet so simple. For making us so smart and capable yet blind to the little things. The nuanced code She designed into the matrix that we are oblivious to. We, or let me say "I" since I can only speak for myself, too often get caught up in the complexities of our world. These fantastically woven multidimensional frameworks that no one is privy to except for us (aka, our overblown and hidden-away egos).

Strip away the layers of pain, fear, numbing, posturing, or whatever fabricated story our ego told us was fact, and we're left with a choice. A choice we made either consciously or unconsciously, yet one that turned fiction into fact. At least for our story. The one we have been building on and telling ourselves for many years.

Seth Godin reminds us that, *"The realest thing in our lives are the stories we invent. We live with these stories, we remind ourselves of them, we perfect them. And, happily, if you don't like the story you're telling yourself, you can change it."*

This is poignant insight into our agency - our ability to act autonomously and freely. The agency we have is not only our most basic human right, but it's also primal. It is innate. It is what connects us to ourselves, God, other humans, and animals. At the core of our agency is choice. Choice over our actions, our thoughts, and our feelings.

As life would have it, the "agency of choice" we have can be quite elusive. It's a slippery little devil that is constantly on the run, hiding from the ego. For the record, the ego despises that you have the power of choice and is deathly afraid that you might use it. Why is that a bad thing? Because when you consciously use your choice for what you know is best for you, the ego loses. He loses the ability to control the situation along with any perceived power he thought he had over choosing for you what is easy, simple, protective, and most likely not in your best interest. And the ego hates change almost as much as he despises choice.

First, we have to build a foundation. A construct we can all agree on to ensure this journey makes sense. Because, on the surface, and I know many of us already know this, not much in this world makes sense. In fact, I may be about to make that worse. For those that prefer tangible unwavering absolutes, I offer my sincere apologies. For the rest of you adventurous folks, we are going to build a framework around what reality is and is not, poke around the edges of where illusions might exist, ask about our own personal delusions, and wrap it up with how all of this can impact emotions and what that means for our feelings, expressed or not.

Simple, easy stuff. Not deep at all. Ha!
My hope is that, through the lens of authenticity, this book will:

- pique your curiosity
- make you question your biases and beliefs
- frustrate the shit out of you
- challenge you to a quick round of fisticuffs
- encourage you to see the real you
- offer you a path forward
- hold your hand as you need it during this journey

After we duke it out and get on the same page, or don't, about the basic tenets of life, my goal is to share the insight and tools necessary for us to stop living under constant unhealthy delusion and, instead, to find a daily practice that incorporates:

Acting with agency: Consciously stepping into choice in our lives. The times when our actions are self-motivated and directed, rather than being relinquished or subject to constraint.

Doing the work: Show up to life. Everyday. Our deepest and most intimate work is also our most inconvenient work. We are worth the effort. Always. And in all ways.
And the work is never over. This is a lifelong journey.

Contribution > Consumption: Create a reality where we have given so much to ourselves that there is an abundance to give to others. A place where we don't need anything, yet we humbly receive the overflowing abundance that others have to offer us. From here, we have absolute authority to create our experiences and live the awe we seek.

--- -- - *Requiem* - -- ---

Hey! Who's at the wheel?
Panic at the loss of control quickly sets in.
Or maybe just a feeling of helplessness?
After all, what can one be expected to do from the passenger seat?
Page 187 of the "Manual of Life" stuck to our noses.
The instructions written with hieroglyphic symbols.
Doing our best to decipher the ancient codex.
To follow the path, a path, whose path?

Lost in our own self-induced tunnel vision.
Causing us to behave in a defective, short-sighted, victimized fashion.
It's time to expand our perspective.
Broaden it. Enhance its clarity. Sharpen the focus.
Seeing, maybe for the first time, the power we have been gifted.
The ability, the agency, the innate human right to choose.
To understand the impact of our choices.
The big ones and the small ones.
Particularly, those we choose not to make.
Compounding. Thickening. Forming an insurmountable mass.
The Jenga stack with too many blocks missing.
Wobbling toward its inevitable demise.
I say NO!
Awaken from the myopic condition that has settled in.
Stop giving away our power and start acting with agency.
It's our birthright after all.
The only gift that God gave equally to each of us.
No one person has an advantage.
We all have the agency,
The agency of choice.
Choice over ourselves.
What we think. What we believe.
How we react. How we show up.
Nobody can take that from us.
Ever.
Unless we give it away.
STOP!
Wake up.

Say "yes."
Own that shit!
With humble gratitude.
The choice has and always will be yours.
Grab the wheel and settle into the driver's seat.
Create your experiences.
Craft your journey.
Passionately indulge in the happiness of pursuit.
And live the awe you seek.

The pinnacle of success here, and in life, is finding happiness, right? Not exactly. I don't believe it can be found. All it takes is a slight shift in mindset, summed up perfectly by one of my favorite quotes from the movie, *Hector and the Search for Happiness*:

"We should concern ourselves, not so much with the pursuit of happiness, but instead, with the happiness of pursuit."

Turns out, the bumps along the road, the setbacks, and the wins are what life is all about. We can't put our finger on happiness because it's all around us, lurking in the corners of everyday life. The curled lip that shows itself for a nanosecond at the last moment of a deep smile. The cool breeze at your back that comes out of seemingly nowhere and everywhere all at once. As we'll find out, happiness is only elusive when we are eager, controlling, and find ourselves straining to put our hands around it.

… PAPERCUTS

Chapter 3:
FINDING REALITY

First and foremost, you and I need to get on the same page. For us to understand and discuss the concepts presented in this book, we need to play around with traditionally esoteric and scientific topics. As we are concerned with non-pathological applications of these concepts, let's agree to have a little fun. To stretch, twist, and rethink definitions, all while paying obeisance to their origins.

This will be fascinating, annoying, and challenging all at once. Yet I believe this framework will provide a solid foundation from which we can operate for the rest of our journey together.

"No one sees reality.
It's worth repeating: No one accurately sees the world as it is.

A person with hearing loss doesn't experience the world the same way a synesthete does. A rock climber doesn't see a steep slope the same way an elderly person does. And an optimist and a pessimist rarely experience opportunities in identical ways.

And each is correct. Correct in that their experience of the world is their experience of the world. It's not possible for anyone to actually see the world as it is.

But there's a significant opportunity we can work toward: To experience the world in a useful way. Not correctly, but ***usefully.***"

- **Seth Godin**

Humans are resilient. We're constantly reinventing ourselves. Pushing forward, retreating, and then making an even bigger push. Gaining ground, slowly, yet always moving forward. Our ability to achieve is almost always directly tied to our ability to believe. When we can envision what the future could look like, we can lock in our goals and drive ourselves toward them.

In our mind, this projection of the future feels tangible. We can taste it, hear the sounds, and smell the grass. Our senses make it real for us. Absolute in a way where belief gets locked in. The secret ingredient is secured and set in place. As belief allows us to know and knowing is what fuels the engine of our reality-creating machine.

Have you ever woken up from a dream and been convinced you were physically there? That at some point you actually visited that place. It was as real as real gets. Possibly even beyond real. The vivid colors and sounds burned into your memory; phantasmagorical, vividly complex, and full of beauty and peace.

We can hope and wish all we want, but in the back of our minds, we know this dream couldn't have been real. Doubt creeps in and we reject the experience as a falsity. None of which prevents us from fantasizing about the possibility, the .001% chance, that "dreams do come true."

Then reality sets in. We scold ourselves for letting our imagination run wild and spending the energy on something that will never happen. We rain on our own parade, becoming our own enthralling party pooper. At best, we offer condolences and hope for the best. At worst, we condemn ourselves for wasting time and energy on such silly things and tell ourselves how stupid we are or that we aren't worthy.

--- -- - *Absolutely Maybe* - -- ---

The best explanation I have seen to describe reality is that it is a mix of facts, truths, and experiences.

Fundamentally, we assume reality refers to a state or quality that is true, actual, or exists independently from the influence of our personal feelings, opinions, perceptions, or imagination. Our understanding of the world is underpinned and anchored by this. It is founded on the idea that an objective reality exists apart from our perceptions or interpretations of it.

For some of us, having this fundamental truth is a necessity. To imagine operating in a world where what we see, feel, smell, or hear isn't absolute and objective can be scary and disturbing. Almost to the point where it's too much to handle. Our brains can glitch out and go haywire when we feel there isn't a common ground that is constant and stable.

That begs the question, is there such a thing as an objective or absolute reality or are these words simply oxymorons?

Scientific theories and models, by their very nature, are subject to verification. Meaning that they can be and often are, over time, proved false or modified. Given the available evidence, scientific knowledge has the best explanations of natural phenomena and is thus provisional and open to constant revision and improvement.

As such, the idea of reality got increasingly complex with the emergence of quantum physics in the early twentieth century when the unusual and seemingly counterintuitive behavior of subatomic particles challenged our traditional conception of what is real. This sparked fresh philosophical arguments over the nature of reality, with some claiming that objective reality is an illusion and that our perceptions and experiences determine our knowledge of the world.

Through his theory of special relativity, Einstein describes how the physical world is nothing but a product of our mind, and the way we perceive and experience reality is subjective. Were this to hold true (maybe it does, maybe it doesn't), then the physical laws governing our world would not be absolute, but dependent on the observer's frame of reference.

Could the physical world simply be a construct of our mind? Are our experiences of reality shaped by our subjective experiences and perspectives? According to Einstein, *"Reality is merely an illusion, albeit a very persistent one."*

Is it all an illusion or could there be more than one reality? The term "duality of reality" is used to describe the view that the world can be broken down into two distinct categories: the physical/material world and the immaterial world of the mind and spirit. This idea can be found in a wide range of religious and philosophical tenets, from Eastern and Western philosophies to some New Age and metaphysical beliefs.

The physical/material dimension of reality is seen as temporary or unreal in some traditions, while the mental/spiritual dimension is seen as more real or permanent. In the Hindu philosophical tradition known as Advaita Vedanta, for instance, the material world is viewed as an illusion called Maya, while the ultimate reality is the eternal, spiritual essence of everything.

The physical and the mental are seen as complementary opposites in some traditions, and the duality of reality is a central tenet in others. In the Western philosophical canon, for instance, René Descartes argued that our mental and physical selves are distinct but interdependent realms, each with its set of characteristics and abilities.

A second way to conceptualize the duality of reality is in terms of the subjective and objective facets of human experience. What we think, feel, and perceive make up the subjective dimension of experience, while the objective dimension consists of the physical world and its attributes.

Another widely accepted theory that challenges the notion of absolute certainty in our knowledge and understanding of reality is Critical Realism. This theory attempts to draw a line between real and observable, claiming that our knowledge and comprehension of the world are founded on the observable—what we can see, touch, smell, taste, and hear. In addition to physicality, it includes what we can sense mentally, emotionally, and spiritually, as well as the perspectives and experiences of other individuals interacting with and contributing to any given situation.

Gestalt theory is yet another viewpoint that shares elements of understanding with both the Theory of Relativity and Critical Realism. It uniquely posits that perception is not a passive process but an active one, shaped by the individual's past experiences, expectations, and cognitive biases, ultimately resulting in different interpretations of the same experiences.

If nothing else, there is a calling here to be open and flexible. Rigidity, whether it be in actions taken or our thinking and belief systems, has no place in our current reality. Our understanding of the universe and all its mechanics is embarrassingly minimal at best. The likelihood that we will fully understand this beautifully complex system called life is comical.

Good! Thank God for that. Fantastic, even!

That said, this leaves me feeling incomplete. Wanting more. Needing to go deeper.

To better comprehend how things work, could it be necessary to break them down into their component parts first? Those that believe in a concept called reductionism certainly think so. When contrasted to the duality of reality, these two schools of thought offer distinct insights into the meaning of life and our place in the universe. The yin and yang of our existence, these two ideas are like two sides of a coin, both vital for a full comprehension of reality.

As we've already discussed, duality of reality is the belief that the world is formed of two complementary and interdependent components, such as mind and matter or wave and particle. On the other hand, reductionism proposes that intricate systems and phenomena can be broken down into their individual parts to better grasp how they work as a whole. It's like figuring out how a clock works by studying the individual gears instead of the whole thing.

Although at first glance these ideas seem diametrically opposed, they balance one another out—if we let them. By integrating these two viewpoints, we can get a more nuanced and fuller picture of reality, like a chef combining sweet and savory flavors to produce a dish that is more than the sum of its parts.

Let's say that we find ourselves in the market for a new watch. As young children, we've always had an appreciation for the aesthetics and craftsmanship of traditional analog watches. We're fascinated by their perceived simplicity and the seemingly magical accuracy of their ability to keep time. The fluidity of their design, both internal and external, is mind-bogglingly awesome. Tiny gears moving in perfect synchronization to create a symphony of ticking and tocking.

"Excuse me," you say to the jeweler behind the counter. *"Can you please take off the back plate and show me how the sprockets are seated? Perfect. And what is the quality control process that the watch goes through at the manufacturer? Would you mind explaining the acceptable manufacturing tolerances for each gear and lever? Excellent. And how can we test and verify this for ourselves? Can we give it a shot right now?"*

Is this the process you need to go through before you buy a watch? Let alone wear it?

How about when you buy a car? A cell phone?

OK, so maybe these are silly or a little extreme. But are they? There are thousands of physical things that we interact with, rely on, trust, and utilize every day that we have no idea exactly how they work. And yet, we have trust, faith, and belief. A knowing.

This is cause for celebration! Because we can and do experience the world in a *useful* way without having to see or understand the world exactly as it is. Or isn't.

--- -- - *Fog of Illusion* - -- ---

"*Hey*," I answered the phone.

"*Hey back*," my friend said and laughed. "*Last night was incredible. Coldplay killed it. They were just fantastic! Between you and me, it might have been the closest thing to a religious experience I've ever had!*"

"*I love that for you!*" was my instinctual reaction. "*But I can't say I feel the same way.*"

"*What?*" my friend said with incredulity. "*Oh my gosh. It was insane for me. The absolute connectedness I felt to every 50,000 walking stories in that stadium all because they had a glowing wristband. My heart felt like it was exploding. I think I cried through 90% of that concert. It was honestly one of the most beautiful things I've ever seen, and it left me with a feeling of home.*"

"*Huh,*" I exhaled. "*Maybe it was how I got unlucky in my seat selection. I ended up having a pole blocking my view half the time. Then the lady next to me wouldn't get off her phone. The guy behind me spilled beer down my back, twice! And the bass was literally pulverizing my chest. It was hard to breathe at times!*"

Does this dichotomy sound familiar?

People construct their own realities from their individual experiences, with no two people having the same experience. Definitely not when it comes to what we smelled, felt, tasted, heard, or felt. We may share similar sentiments about what the experience was like and the impact it had on us, yet the result of our experiences could've been and most likely were very different from each other.

Now I'm curious. Is there any evidence for a universally shared reality?

Thinking, Fast and Slow, by psychologist Daniel Kahneman, examines how people's thoughts and perceptions are formed and how they might differ from reality (he assumes a universally shared reality exists). Kahneman claims that there are two distinct modes of mental processing going on in every person's head: System 1, which is quick, intuitive, and automatic; and System 2, which is more methodical, deliberate, and aware. Kahneman contends that these two systems interact to make sense of the environment.

Kahneman's work is limited to explaining the cognitive processes of how and why we make certain decisions. While valuable in the framework it provides, he stops short on how we use our different experiences, emotions, and beliefs together to form a coherent sense of ourselves and our individual realities.

Very few things in our world are straightforward. Our realities are built around facts and truths. Facts are few and far between and subject to being challenged and proved otherwise. Leaving facts as only absolute until an alternate hypothesis is tested and trumps the current one. Truths, on the other hand, are polluted and only apply to whoever speaks or holds them. I can only speak for myself here, but this means challenging my long-held understanding of what I thought a truth was, making it subjective at best.

This leaves us on shaky ground. People, places, and things are rarely as they seem.

Especially people.

Are we all going crazy? Are we designed to function this way? How can we know what's up and what's down? My head is spinning.

Let's look at things from a different angle. The desk I am typing this from is made of wood and metal. The coffee cup off to my left-hand side is double-wall aluminum to keep in the heat. These things are real. They exist. Where things get mushy is when we try to describe our interactions with these objects.

Me: My desk has a smooth finish on it, not too shiny and was cut geometrically with a saw, so it looks manufactured. It acts as a firm writing surface but the edges are soft. The arms of my chair are constantly putting dent marks on the edges as I rotate throughout the day. The desk is not of the highest quality, so I don't put anything too heavy on it. It does the job and looks nice, though. Oh, and my coffee stains wipe right off. That's a must-have for me!

My daughter: My dad's desk is meh. It looks good, I guess. He yells at me when I sit on it. I guess that's because we heard a cracking noise once when I was sitting on it. It's too low for me to sit on my knees in the chair and still roll underneath it.

Same object. Completely different experiences.

The fog of illusion slowly rolls in.

According to the Cambridge Dictionary, an illusion is something that is not as it seems, and a delusion is something a person believes and wants to be true, when it is actually not true.

Truth, it turns out, is a tricky word. More on that later.

Multiple other sources agree that an illusion is a false perception of reality, often caused by the brain interpreting sensory information incorrectly. Okay. Full stop. This is where I see serious problems with this argument and with language in general. Who is the deciding voice on whether my sensory system is interpreting things incorrectly? There is so much wiggle room in the definitions here that it gets me all riled up.

I can't remember the last time I was in a room with a group of people where every single person felt, through their senses, that the room was either too hot or too cold, too loud or too crowded, and everyone agreed. How can we possibly say that one person is right and the rest wrong? You might be shivering from being cold at a temperature of 72 degrees when the guy next to you is sweating bullets. Everything we sense is on a spectrum. A sliding scale with no absolutes. There is no one way or one-size-fits-all.

Stepping off that soap box, let's get back to our exploration of possibilities. Society claims that a delusion, on the other hand, is a fixed belief that is not supported by reality. While illusions can be temporary and harmless (they have to be, since living in the present, moment by moment, makes the illusion we call life extremely temporary), delusions can have a significant impact on a person's thoughts, emotions, and behavior.

From a clinical perspective, self-delusion is when someone convinces themselves of something that is not necessarily true or holds onto a belief despite contradicting evidence. Sometimes thought of as a form of self-deception, where someone is unwilling or unable to accept the truth about a situation or circumstance. This can be harmful, as it can lead us to make decisions based on false information or to ignore important facts that may be relevant to our well-being. There is a flip side to this, as self-delusion can also serve as a coping mechanism, allowing us to maintain a sense of hope or optimism in difficult situations.

And to throw more confusion on the table, according to Wikipedia (on the day I wrote this, anyways), *"A delusion is a false fixed belief that is not amenable to change in light of conflicting evidence, [which] is distinct from a belief based on false or incomplete information, [such as an] illusion or some other misleading effects of perception…"*

Let's not forget that illusions are always temporary. They are an experience (effect of perception) in the here and now. The present. If we are remembering them or foreshadowing them, then they can only be delusions. The past is already gone and the future isn't here yet, making them both nonexistent.

Personally, I struggle with all the different definitions that exist as they repetitively contradict themselves. If not in isolation, especially so when applied to a specific situation. Maybe it's because they're attempting to be absolute. It could also be because I like to challenge the status quo. Or maybe we just can't accept these definitions at face value anymore.

Let's apply this to the Coldplay concert story and see if we can rectify what happened. What was real and whose experience is an accurate depiction of reality?

You don't know? Yeah, me neither.

The only logical conclusion is that two truths exist simultaneously. The only way that's possible is that the stories themselves are a delusion because there are no facts behind them. Each story has to do with our individual experiences of the same illusion.

It would be wise to remember that our perceptions and interpretations of events are influenced by a variety of elements, including prior experiences, cultural contexts, and emotions. None of these are shared equivocally between the two of us, let alone the human population.

Now that we have a firm grasp on things and these concepts are all cleared up, let's muddy the waters. I mean, why not add a little more confusion to the mix? Henri Michaux tells us, *"The reality of the other person is not in what he reveals to you, but in what he cannot reveal to you."*

One of my daily rituals is to read from *The Book of Awakening* by Mark Nepo. It regularly provides the perfect little nugget of wisdom, in under 90 seconds, that sets the stage for a good day. The following short story made me close my eyes and laugh. It's almost like Mark got in my head when he wrote this:

"It reminds me of a friend who had a flat tire on a country road. After finding he had no jack, he began walking, hoping to find a nearby farmer who would help him. It was getting dark and the crickets were getting louder. As he walked the overgrown road, he began to throw the dice of worry in his mind: What if the farmer's not home? What if he is and won't let me use his jack? What if he won't let me use his phone? What if he is frightened of me? I never did anything to him! Why won't he just let me use his phone?!

By the time he knocked on the farmer's door, my friend was so preoccupied with what could go wrong that when the friendly old man answered, my friend bellowed, 'Well, you can keep your Goddamn jack!'"

--- -- - *Periscopes of Perception* - -- ---

My dad was in the Navy and did his tours in Vietnam on a submarine. He used to tell my brother and me stories about being out in the middle of the ocean, stuck underwater for weeks at a time. Talk about becoming delusional! I can't even imagine.

As an officer, one of his jobs was to man the periscope. His nightly duty came calling every evening that they surfaced to charge the batteries. His was an old diesel model, which meant this was an almost nightly affair.

Periscopes always struck me as such an odd invention. They're the definition of myopic—built to see one small area of the world at a time, always in a horizontal plane, never above or below. What a restricted view of life this portrays. It leaves the viewer to decipher reality out of limited information and lots of assumptions.

We are plagued with a myopic view of the world as well. You can't see through her eyes or experience life inside his body, which turns out to be quite limiting. But not for us! We can assume that how we experience something must be similar for others. And we do just that. Casually tossing aside any regard or concern for how insensitive and wrong we might be.

When two witnesses experience the same event, a particular circumstance could appear positive to one person while bringing on feelings of despair to another, and both may think that their interpretation is the only accurate one. In this situation, both parties are suffering from myopic self-delusion. There is absolutely nothing wrong with it as long as it doesn't turn into a belief that one side or the other is the only valid point of view. This is when things can potentially take a turn toward the unhealthy, fostering a negative outlook and perception about life and who we are.

If instead, we opt to embrace change, acquire knowledge, and stay open to being wrong, then we keep the door to possibility cracked open. As we reflect back on our experiences, and are inspired by novel viewpoints, our ideas and interpretations often evolve over time. A common occurrence in the political arena is when someone thinks a particular political philosophy is the absolute truth, but after participating in conversations and learning about various points of view, their beliefs shift. This emphasizes the ephemeral nature of truth and the value of being receptive to fresh ideas and information.

A mistaken perception of reality can also result from a pillowcase (turned rucksack) of skeletons that many of us carry around and regularly swing up and plop on the table. Confirmation bias is one such skeleton, which is the propensity to seek out information that supports one's preexisting ideas while ignoring information that challenges them. We have lots of these biases that we carry with us while also pretending they are our friends. It's all bullshit, though. That bag of old bones rarely, if ever, serves us well.

In light of this, there could be a counterargument suggesting that self-delusion is generally not a valid concept. Given that a person's perspective and interpretation of their experiences determine whether a belief is true, it's quite possible that self-delusion may just be a delusion in and of itself!

I want to introduce you to a friend of mine, Jonas Nordstrom. This intro is a little lengthy but necessary to give the proper insight into who this man is. He is an adjunct professor at the School of Social Work at Arizona State University (ASU), holds a doctorate in transpersonal psychology and esoteric studies, and is currently pursuing a second doctorate in clinical psychology. He has lived and worked in war-torn countries like Afghanistan, Kosovo, Israel, and Egypt, as well as providing trauma relief workshops and crisis support programs in India, Kenya, United Arab Emirates, Great Britain, Spain, Switzerland, the Netherlands, Germany, Denmark, Norway, Sweden, and Finland. Jonas also served five years in one of the Swedish Special Forces, with deployments to the Balkans and Afghanistan.

If that wasn't enough, he also had a stint working as a yoga teacher in India and trained with the Swedish Olympic weightlifting team. Jonas is a badass human being, husband, father, friend, and is a wealth of knowledge. We had frequent conversations over the last year, and I have woven the relevant pieces throughout this book.

Jonas: *"When you think about delusions, do you think they're always a negative thing or do you think they could be positive?"*

Brent: *"Both, I suppose. I mean, why not? This is a huge part of what this conversation is about after all. It's talking about all of these things. But yes, I think they could be and likely are both positive and negative."*

Jonas: *"As long as it serves your purposes and helps your life, it could be positive. For instance, if it temporarily helped you get through a trauma or a loss."*

Brent: *"And maybe, if this (life) is all an illusion, then our point of view, or the story we choose to believe and lock in, is always a delusion."*

Jonas: *"Yes. I see. Two things. First, I would say a positive delusion could be a defense mechanism that helps us to get through certain experiences. A good example here is a divorce. It's painful and we have defense mechanisms, but then, over time, our story (the delusion) changes. If we look at illusion from the standpoint of Einstein, that everything is an illusion, albeit a persistent one, this then becomes the trick that our senses play on us. That we think reality is real just because we perceive it in a certain way. Where the color red could be slightly or drastically different for you than it is for me. And yet, we'll never really know as we can't empirically test this."*

The depth of our stories, of our experiences, are nothing but epic. It's no wonder we seek out talk therapy and get stuck on a couch for 10 years, making no real progress as there are too many layers to get through. The density of the web we've been spinning since childhood is overwhelming. Paralyzing.

Yet we push forward. To what end are we engaging in this search? Do we honestly believe that there is one event, one experience, or one moment that all of our pain is tied back to? And if we somehow put our finger on this singular event, we would know, once and for all, just know!

This seems so enticing when we first consider it. Almost like knowing what the event is would give us the power to solve it. And it might. Awareness is the first step on any journey. It all starts here. The fallacy is that there is ONE event. A singular moment that started it all.

When we back away from the periscope, allowing our eyes to adjust, and our brain to reconnect to both eyeballs, our vision shifts back into the 3D world. It's at this moment that clear and peripheral vision snaps back into place. Then we see it clear as day.

There is no one thing.

--- -- - *Parallel Perspectives* - -- ---

Ding! A new text had arrived.

"*Hey Brent! Can you grab coffee before our kid's basketball game on Thursday?*" asked my friend Tim.

"*Sure. Let's meet an hour before the game and then we can head over together,*" was my snappy reply.

"*Perfect. Thank you!*" Tim gushed.

"*Of course. See you then,*" I said with finality.

It turned out that Tim was concerned about the annual review that just landed in his email inbox. His motivation for inviting me to coffee was so that we could catch up on life and our kids, and he could pick my brain to get my perspective on his review.

Tim showed up exactly on time. Being a stickler myself (or neurotic?), I appreciate this quality in other people. We both ordered an iced coffee with a splash of oat milk. The barista thought that was "cute." We smirked and rolled our eyes at each other.

Tim and I have an easy friendship. We don't hang out much, but when we do, conversation flows and we can go deep quickly. As we grabbed the last two comfy leather chairs, our conversation started midair before my butt even hit the seat. We started discussing the merits of different strategies as it pertained to completing the self-assessment portion of his review. One question in particular moved us to explore it deeper. It asked, "What didn't work, and what would you change or do differently next year?'"

Immediately Tim imagined this to be a question about his performance. His specific role in some situations, although he was unaware of it, didn't go well. I watched him go deep, internally processing a feeling that must have just washed over him.

His eyes hollowed, and I beckoned him back to our conversation. With a quick shake of the head, not dissimilar to a dog getting the water off its back, his eyes shot over and locked back in with mine.

"Tim," I looked at him with a faint squint. *"What if this question isn't about you?"*

"What do you mean? Of course, this is about me. It's a self-assessment," he fired back.

"Yes. Yes, it is. But does that mean it's only about you? Could it also be about your perspective on things? Asking you to share how things went over the last year from the unique experiences you had, within the larger construct of the team?" I inquired.

He sat there for a moment and, with a look of pleasant bewilderment, said, *"Man, I never thought of it that way. By gosh, you could be right!"*

"It's not about finding right or wrong, Tim," I retorted. *"It's about understanding the nuances of the question. That there doesn't have to be one interpretation."*

We spent the next ten minutes or so discussing the possible angles of attack and what would align with his journey and values. That's when I had an idea and offered, "If you were your boss or the other company executives, what would you want? What would add the most value to them and their decision-making in the future? Is it for you to throw yourself under the bus? To be self-deprecating? Or to share where the processes broke down? Where the team didn't embrace the concept of teamwork. To shine a light on a shadow they didn't know existed?"

I could see that Tim was still struggling to embrace this alternate perspective of the reality he thought was absolute when we walked into this coffee shop ten minutes ago. I reminded him that he had an employment contract, had not broken any rules, was performing above expectations from a numbers standpoint, and was an equity partner. There was nothing negative that could come out of this assessment.

That's when something shifted. A gear connected with a sprocket and they locked in place together. Grinding through the friction of moving something from a standstill, momentum started to build. He got it and was re-evaluating the story he had previously told himself.

Allowing for multiple interpretations to exist opened up a plethora of possibilities. It exposed the illusion in front of him. Reality became a dirty word. The question now was, "Whose reality?" Tim's realization and understanding of the delusion he had embraced allowed him to take another look at the situation. He was now aware of the illusory nature of what was in front of him.

Another take on how we create a "sense of self" is explored in the book, *The Self Illusion: How the Social Brain Creates Identity* by Bruce Hood. The sense of self, it is argued, is an illusion created by the brain, and that the brain creates this illusion by connecting different experiences, emotions, and beliefs together to form a coherent sense of self. Bruce concludes that, *"We have an illusion of unity and consistency because our brains construct a coherent self-narrative to make sense of our experiences."*

This provides both frightening and promising insight. The idea that we are consistent and stable in who we are as humans, is nothing but an illusion. A self-created illusion (or delusion) at that. In reality, the self is dynamic and constantly evolving through interactions, experiences, and our social environment. It is up to us to increase our self-awareness and embrace the natural and healthy state of flux that exists. Then, and only then, can we take back our power by exercising our agency of choice.

The truly exciting part about this is that nothing about us is constant. We have full control, absolute choice, to decide who and what we show up to life as. And tomorrow we can choose differently. No one can stop or change this, as the power to do so lies squarely in our hands.

--- -- - *Trustworthy* - -- ---

"It's different to feel truth for ourselves versus thinking that it's true for everyone."
- **Jonas Nordstrom**

Even if our perception and interpretation of reality are subjective, that does not necessarily indicate that the reality we experience is entirely illusory or that the concept of a true reality is false. Our experiences and vantage points can still provide us with valuable and instructive insights, even when they don't perfectly reflect reality. These different viewpoints, when we allow them to coexist, impact our experiences and how we might learn to see things from multiple perspectives. We gain depth from our understanding. A discernment that earns us a more accurate picture of reality.

Trust does not have to be elusive either.

Brent: *"Jonas, you just touched on what I think is the number one way that we hurt ourselves."*

Jonas *"Yes. We want certainty and for things to not change. Even though that is against nature, as everything in nature is constantly changing. It grows until it dies. But the ego doesn't want that, because it likes to understand a process. So, we want certainty, and when we freeze the natural flow of things, we don't want to recognize that there is an illusion or delusion. We just want to believe that what I know is true, so I don't need to complicate things."*

Brent: *"This is the place where we create so much arguing, frustration, and misunderstanding in society because we forget that everything is subjective in regard to our interactions with the world. Yet, we then take our truth, and we hold so firmly to it, getting frustrated when it's also not your truth is commonly the outcome. And that is such a hard lesson."*

Jonas: *"Relationships are where it is most common to have this friction. Because that's where we think we are the same or we see things the same, and then that's where we get so complicated."*

Brent: *"Yes, with our significant others and with our kids. I know that someday I want to be able to have this conversation with my kids. To tell them I was wrong. That I approached things incorrectly. I know I tried to put my truth on them all the time, instead of allowing for their own truths to coexist with mine."*

Jonas: *"You did what you thought was best at that time."*

Brent: *"This is the overriding thing, and this is what will allow me to be human and talk about tough things in this book. I believe, at all times, we are doing what we think is the best thing. That, right there, is what I believe will help us all find, not forgiveness necessarily, but a deep sense of connection and empathy for the rest of the world."*

Jonas: *"At least an understanding and empathy within the story someone has told themselves. The delusion they are stuck in, then what they did makes sense. When it comes to contemplating truth in regard to how to deal with our own life and make personal choices, I often reflect on the idea that it's different perceiving a truth subjectively, which is deeply personal and hopefully, but not always, works for us individually, versus assuming that this subjective truth is an absolute one applicable universally. So, truth as an* *individually guided navigation system versus absolute universal objectivity. From a psychological perspective, realizing that you're always in subjectivity and that we are never really reaching a state of fully understanding truth. We are just getting closer to the truth."*

When it comes to making choices or developing relationships, it is not always necessary for us to have conclusive evidence or complete assurance. Even if we do not have all of the knowledge or proof we would want, we are still able to make decisions based on our gut feelings, the things we believe to be true, and the trust we have in alternative possibilities.

The danger here is when we feel our perception of the world is wholly accurate and then discover that others' perceptions differ, sometimes wildly, from ours. It can be easy to conclude that they are the ones who are prejudiced, skewed, uneducated, ignorant, unreasonable, or wicked.

A quick scroll through just about any social media platform proves this as self-evident and contagious. It's overwhelming. Billions of us worldwide are hooked on this dopamine-inducing phenomenon. At the risk of diminishing this enormous problem, I won't spend any more time here. The negative potential that is oozing out of our phones and into our fingers is real. Implicitly, we all know it.

Engage with eyes wide open. Understand that most of what we consume online is *not* reality. Not as we were meant to experience it. And, paradoxically, truth is *very* elusive in this virtual realm. Particularly when we start to dig deeper into our own truth.

This holds as true for everyone we interact with as it does for ourselves. Trust, as with all things, starts on the inside. If we don't trust ourselves, we can't truly trust anyone else. The container required for trust is based on our understanding of what truth means for us. If we have no trust and no personal truths, it is impossible to understand and trust others.

Because truth lives on a spectrum, a sliding scale, it is imperative that we have a grasp on what it means to trust ourselves first. To get comfortable with the gray area where truth and trust reside. If this is a new concept for you, I get that it sounds a bit scary. Cage rattling even. But unless you live inside of an Excel spreadsheet, there really are no absolutes.

Deep down, we know this. A world without absolutes is a universal truth, if there is such a thing. It is the element of belief, faith even, that distinguishes truth from fact. How can we get comfortable with that notion if we don't have faith in our deepest, darkest intentions?

At our core, I believe (yes, I hold this as one of my truths) that we are all doing our best, all the time. Sure, it may come through in destructive and nasty ways, but it is never directly on purpose. We are not built to hurt for hurting's sake. We hurt to make ourselves feel better. And while this doesn't justify or make certain behavior acceptable, it speaks to our intentions of no longer feeling pain or fear. Right or wrong, we make choices to protect ourselves, despite the harm it brings to others. In its own backward way, we trust that our actions, our choices, are the best ones we can make at any given time in order to keep ourselves safe. So says the ego, anyways.

It's our truth. Shitty and hurtful, yes, at times, but truth, nonetheless. And this trust runs deep. It's why talk therapy can take many years to make a significant breakthrough. We trust ourselves so deeply that we can't fathom an alternative. An outside truth that contradicts our closest-held internal truths.

Brené Brown has impeccable insight on this topic. She shared, *"Trust is not about perfection. It's about giving someone the benefit of the doubt and being willing to take a risk based on the potential for a positive outcome."*

How can we possibly trust others and have any faith that they will do the right thing?

First off, what is the "right thing"?

Second, why do you trust yourself?

In some ways, it's like opting for the devil you know versus the one you don't. Neither of them is absolutely true nor accurate. Yet we have a level of comfort and understanding with one of them. Even if they are not as honorable or often choose differently than we would want them to. Their predictability feels safe, making them an easy choice.

The phrase, "living one's truth," takes on a whole new meaning. In that vein, so does trusting others. Trust is not the same as nor is it based on truth. Truths are not facts. Facts don't determine our reality.

The question remains, who and what is worth the calculated risk of us giving our trust to?

--- -- - *Final Framework* - -- ---

If you aren't at least slightly confused, had your personal constitution rattled, or are struggling to understand what's been real in your life, the following perspective from, New York Times Best Selling author and spiritual teacher, Gary Zukav should do the trick:

"Reality is what we take to be true. What we take to be true is what we believe. What we believe is based upon our perceptions. What we perceive depends upon what we look for. What we look for depends upon what we think. What we think depends upon what we perceive. What we perceive determines what we believe. What we believe determines what we take to be true. What we take to be true is our reality."

The reality (ha, I love double meanings) is that there is no universal reality. At least not one that we can collectively understand and agree to from a human perspective. In the effort to find a common ground, I propose that we adopt the following construct to serve as the framework that we can push and pull, stretch and condense, all of the forthcoming conversations from.

The **physical world** is tangible and real; however, one cannot experience it as absolute. Each of us can only understand the physical world through our experience of it. As humans, we experience life through our five senses. This leads to each person having a different interpretation and understanding of what the physical world is for them.

Our interaction with **reality** is, therefore, in the eye of the beholder. Each of our experiences is truly an illusion. Which leaves our individual **stories**, the interpretations of our experiences, to be nothing but delusions. And our **truths** are based on our understanding of these stories.

In summary, we construct stories and beliefs (past and future) based on our interactions and experiences (present) with a world that is not as it seems, leading to the creation of truths that we each hold as a wholly accurate representation of life, and the basis for where we place our trust.

The core formula thus becomes: *Perception of reality = Delusion of the illusion*

Which, in simpler terms, is to say that what we perceive to be real is no more than the story we tell ourselves about our experiences. Everything boils down to our in-the-moment interpretation of what we see, feel, hear, taste, and touch, including other extra-sensory inputs.

If this is true, which we have already agreed that it is, at least for the remainder of our time reading this book together, then why are we not constructing the most fantastic stories of joy, happiness, and love for ourselves?

Why are we not teaching our young to become creators instead of discoverers?

Contributors instead of consumers? To design their futures by being owners of the present?

It's time to wake up and be present. To show up fully aware. As awareness is a doorway. A threshold we need to cross in order to step into our power.

The lost power of …

PAPERCUTS

Chapter 4:
WAKING UP

--- -- - *Sleepwalking* - -- ---

Chapter One
I walk down the street.
There is a deep hole in the sidewalk.
I fall in.
I am lost... I am helpless.
It isn't my fault.
It takes forever to find a way out.

Chapter Two
I walk down the same street.
There is a deep hole in the sidewalk.
I pretend I don't see it. I fall in again.
I can't believe I am in the same place.
But it isn't my fault.
It still takes me a long time to get out.

Chapter Three
I walk down the same street.
There is a deep hole in the sidewalk.
I see it is there. I still fall in...
It's a habit...but, my eyes are open.
I know where I am. It is my fault.
I get out immediately.

Chapter Four
I walk down the same street.
There is a deep hole in the sidewalk.
I walk around it.

Chapter Five
I walk down another street.

- **Portia Nelson**, *There's a Hole in My Sidewalk*

We've all fallen into our own metaphorical hole at some point in our lives. After reading this story, it's a fairly safe bet that a part of you resonated with the feelings it evoked. Yet we have a tendency to stay on the surface. To "get it" but not truly understand it, or to know it yet fail to integrate it.

When we get present, and take a deeper look, we find that God and the universe are spitting their wit at us, with a side of sarcasm. They are tapping us on our shoulder (or slugging us in the solar plexus) saying,

"Do you see this? Do you understand the correlation? You are a highly evolved cosmic being and yet you keep choosing the same outcome, over and over. It's your choice. Always has been. Are you ready to learn and move on yet? No? Okay, no judgment here. Enjoy the walk."

--- -- - *A Special Gift* - -- ---

"I suspect many haven't even considered that they have a choice in their stories."

- **Rebecca Heiss, PhD**, *Fear[less]*

The one thing we've all been gifted without prejudice is free will. Many of us understand and exercise this, albeit at too high of a level for what I am referring to. Free will typically shows up something like: I want to go out for sushi tonight, I'm voting straight down the Democratic party line, I'm never wearing a tie again, or Buddha is the path that resonates with me.

What I'm referring to here is **agency of choice**, which tends to be much more granular. Subatomic level granular. Choices that are, at times, consciously made, though often they are not.

The unhealthy side to how they show up can look like:
- she was looking at me funny and therefore (the choice is the assumption made) she must not like me very much
- he didn't respond to my text for 18 hours which means he's hiding something
- something as simple as telling ourselves, "Everyone thinks I'm weird"
- choosing to believe we'll never be able to take that trip to Italy
- a boy like that will never like a girl like me

When these choices happen unconsciously, it's often because of the patterns we've programmed ourselves with. The real choice is so overwhelming that we've told ourselves we just don't care, or we have previously chosen a particular way, so we lock in the programming and put it on autopilot (because it feels safer somehow). Our crafty ego knows that this new choice could puncture part of our story's silky web, and we couldn't possibly put the foundation of our global self at risk.

It can be terrifying. I get it!

Contemplating the idea of being or doing it wrong for the last however many years of our lives can be overwhelming. We can go back in time, replay every memory, and run it through the fun game of What-If Roulette, torturing ourselves incessantly and unnecessarily. In the end, we come to the realization that there was never only one choice and that any number of them could have drastically changed the course of life.

The past is the past. It's gone. History. It's been written. C'est la vie. Sayonara!

Eckhart Tolle said it best, *"The past has no power over the present moment, only power over your mind."*

In Victor Frankl's *Man's Search for Meaning*, he states, *"Everything can be taken from a man but one thing: the last of the human freedoms—to choose one's attitude in any given set of circumstances, to choose one's own way."*

Another stalwart on this subject, Dr. David Hawkins, echoed these sentiments when he said, *"The past is a memory, the future is a projection. The present is a gift, that is why it is called the present."*

This makes my heart smile every time I read this.
How many of us treat the present moment, each moment, as a special gift?

I sure don't. Not often enough anyways. I'm lucky if I can embrace the current moment a handful of times per day. And that's not a judgment or guilt trip on myself. It's just reality. Even though it's impossible to thank the present moment 86,400 times a day, it can be something that we come back to in the moments we question things. When the past or future bogs us down. The moments when accepting and receiving what is in front of us feels like the most painful option. It's at these focal points that a quick reminder of what a special gift being present, in the here and the now, truly is.

The best part about our worst moments? Choice exists beyond the pain, bringing with it a sense of levity. It strips away the seriousness that we originally wrote and hard-coded our story with and challenges us to reassess. To break the shackles of the past. To choose differently now. Because there is only now and *now* is where your power lies.

The gift of choice.
The power of choice.

Existing always and **only** in the now. The present moment. This present moment.

REMINDER: Our freedom ends where someone else's begins. In other words, we have complete agency of choice except where it infringes on the rights or freedoms of others. Of course, you are an adult and can do whatever the heck you want. While the choice is yours to make, there are very real consequences that follow.

--- -- - *Distractions* - -- ---

Something is out of place. That nagging feeling we sometimes get. A nudge or maybe a zing in our gut. An internal wire that gets tripped if a choice flies in the face of the current image we hold about ourselves. "I've thought this way for at least ten years. It's worked for me before and my friends have confirmed that they agree with me." Sound familiar?

It's why we, as a society (yes, I'm generalizing), have designed and deployed so many options to keep us distracted, numb, or tuned out. They prevent us from having to feel anything. At least anything of real value.

Here's a top 20 list:

1.	Social media	11.	Music and dancing
2.	Television and movies	12.	Travel
3.	Video games	13.	Hobbies
4.	Shopping	14.	Reading/writing
5.	Sex	15.	Religion or spirituality
6.	Gambling	16.	Volunteering
7.	Food	17.	Pets
8.	Alcohol and drugs	18.	Fashion and beauty
9.	Work	19.	Technology and gadgets
10.	Exercise	20.	Home improvement projects

Of course, some, if not many on this list can be healthy and positive. It's the mindless use or abuse of them that we're talking about. Those moments when we choose a number from the list to conveniently escape the present.

What does a football game, three beers, and a little sex have in common?

They are our favorite ways to give away our choice or shove it down to the depths of our internal processing where automatic programming can take over.

Reality Check! Now that half of you reading this are cursing the page, let's clear the air.

There's nothing wrong with football or any professional sport. Taking the occasional break to shut our brain down, find camaraderie, and yell at the screen is healthy. At the same time, obsession with anything can be extremely destructive. In ALL the ways. What's particularly harmful is the level of distraction that leads to a lack of presence.

Beer has been our friend for millennia. Until it hasn't. Alcohol lubricates conversations and social interactions, and too much can numb us from head to toe and heart to soul. Even in small doses, the way alcohol lubricates is by numbing. It targets our ego, so we give less of a shit. Which is sometimes just what the doctor ordered. I get it! Until the self-loathing of tomorrow comes knocking.

Sex is arguably the most fantastic part of being human: connection, vulnerability, generosity, compassion, confidence, spirituality, and pure dopamine-pumping pleasure. It's also an easy go-to to mask the reality of things, potentially leading to an unhealthy addiction. Those feel-good chemicals can also give us a false sense that "everything's great" until they wear off and we're left with an empty and deflated feeling. That connection we were seeking was only just scratching the surface of what we truly desired.

The challenge here is that we can get overwhelmed with life and these three options, whether used by themselves or stacked together, can be used as an escape pod. Climb in. Shut the door. Eject!

Silence. Our choice is gone, but so is the pain. Ah, it's worth it, though.

Drugs are another appealing option for a reason. They give us a different kind of escape pod. Cocaine, for one, is phenomenal. Talk about feeling AMAZING. I was a superhero every time those chemicals got absorbed through my septum. I became smarter than I've ever been before and better looking. Nothing stood in my way. *Nothing.* And problems, challenges, setbacks, ha! I spat at these simple things that were only for suckers.

If being present is the metric, cocaine falls on about the 5-yard line. It's almost impossible to hear, see, or feel other people when those molecules are floating in our veins. The best part about this drug is also the worst, as it brings all the pleasure and all the attention onto and into oneself. Human-to-human connection is severed as narcissism settles in. Free will is highly in focus and at our fingertips, ready to deploy, but our agency of choice has evaporated.

The euphoric high is the best, until it fades. Generously, that's about two hours. Then it's the worst. We lose connection to ourselves. Depression comes quickly, as humans weren't designed to not have a connection to themselves or others. Our system shuts down and puts us into hibernation mode, locking down all of our programs until we can reconnect and eventually find our way back to ourselves.

It's a destructive cycle. Yes, it works, and quickly too. The speed of it is arguably its magnetism.

Whatever your pleasure is here or your go-to way to avoid yourself and ignore your agency, it matters not. Strip away the societal rating system we have on which of these modalities is better or worse, acceptable or not, legal or illegal, they all accomplish the same task. You no longer have to consciously choose. The irony is we end up making two choices when this happens.

1. No choice, which ends up becoming a choice for whatever decision(s) we've previously made. Falling under the *"don't fix it if it ain't broken"* adage. Simple, easy, safe…spineless.

2. It also becomes a choice not to put oneself first. This ends up becoming one of the most common and deepest papercuts. Not choosing ourselves keeps us on the path to a slow and painful death.

Either of these subconscious choices represent the easy approach. They also artificially relieve us of any accountability. Consciously exercising our choice is the path to the best solution, but it is not for the faint of heart. Carrying the burden of accountability is real. Of course, it exists equally for all our choices. We just like to pretend it's not there when we don't choose consciously.

I had the privilege of meeting a gentleman by the name of Preston Smiles recently during a workshop on emotional intelligence. It's no wonder he is considered a master at his craft, as his charisma and intuition are off the charts. Shortly thereafter, I picked up his book *Now or Never* and found this little gem:

"We are responsible for our experience of the event—no matter how undesirable or beautiful it may be. We can choose the experience of fear, doubt, and blame, or we can choose to release blame altogether and choose the experience of a new perspective, a lesson, a gift... In the situations we can't control, we can control how we respond to them."

--- -- - *Why Is Not the Question* - -- ---

Thanksgiving rolled in just like any other year. It was a smaller gathering than the grand galas of past years, but a good turnout, nonetheless. Uncle Ed told stories of great grandma's escapades as a young woman pioneering the West and women's rights and how that landed her in jail more than once. Something she was all too proud of too and had become her calling card in her later years. Who can blame her? She was a wild spirit who always lived life to the fullest, pushing boundaries and proving everyone wrong, at every juncture.

Ed had that same gusto and passion for life. He lived in Alaska for half a year in a small cabin, surviving off the land, then retreating to his fancy Miami lifestyle in the winter. The dichotomy was laughable yet beyond intriguing.

Ed's brother, Al, could've been the mailman's if you know what I mean (from a different, unknown father). That spirit and "chase" that was passed down to Ed skipped right over Al. And it was awkward at times. The polarity between them was repellent. In more than one way. When they were in a room together, an incoherent vibration floated through the air.

This year it smacked me square in the face. Something more was afoot. All of my senses were screaming at me. It was like system overload. Everything went haywire.

I pulled Ed aside and he ushered me into the living room, where we took a seat on two crusty, burnt orange high-back reading chairs. He put his hand on my arm and said, *"It's not good. Al's in bad shape. He has taken a turn for the worse and they say it doesn't look promising."*

"Ugh," I grunted. *"How is Claire?"* Claire was Al's daughter and also my cousin.

"She knows. It's all still soaking in, though," Ed said with raised eyebrows and furrowed brow. That look of reality mixed with sadness after having accepted the inevitable. His shoulders shrugged in coordination with a deep breath and a heavy sigh.

Not wanting to be a downer for the rest of the festivities, I let the conversation be, leaving it idle until we could pick it back up at another time.

I had all the best intentions to reach out to Claire the following week. Time, being the trickster that it is, had Christmas Eve upon us before I could even blink. I stopped procrastinating and immediately texted Claire. We offered the standard "merrys & happys" and set a time to meet for coffee and get caught up three days later. She didn't know what Ed had told me, and yet, how could she not know that I had to know something? Only those relatives who were too drunk to pay attention could have missed the obvious state Al was in.

"Hey sweetie," she said warmly as we embraced in a long hug.

"Claire, you look, calm?" I stammered, half expecting her to appear panicked.

"Uh, yeah. Sure. What does that mean exactly?"

"Well, I just, I'm…"

"Yes, it's about my Dad. Sucks. This is probably his last Christmas with us."

"I'm so sorry! This is all so sudden. Are you okay?"

We trailed off into small talk as we stood at the counter waiting for our hot beverages. Coffee in hand, we found an unoccupied corner of the cafe and made ourselves comfortable.

Claire dove in, sharing, *"We thought this might be the last Christmas with Dad. And you know my work. They expect us to treat our job like nothing is more important and we would sacrifice anything to help out. But this holiday was different. I made it very clear that I wasn't going to work, and I made that announcement a month ahead of time.*

This was going to be a family-focused holiday. With so many unknowns surrounding my dad, I felt that I needed to be intentional this year. Of course, I get a call on Christmas Eve from the Regional Manager. Two other people had called out sick and he, in plain words, made it clear that I needed to work on Christmas. I stayed calm and explained to him all that was going on. He listened and then said, 'Well, you know, the choice is, of course, yours.' And the way he said it was, you either choose your family or you choose this job. He made it implicitly clear that if I chose not to work, then I would likely lose my job.

And, so, what did I do? I went to work. I told myself, 'You have no choice.' I felt like I had to do this. I had to go to work. And I made a choice. Right? I know that I had a choice. I could have said, 'No.' I mean this might have been the last Christmas that I ever get to spend with my father.

There are 158 million restaurant jobs out there. I know I would just get another one, but I potentially won't get another Christmas with my father. With my family all together. Right? So I made this choice that moment, thinking that I had no choice. But I made one. You know, so how is that not a choice? When I explain it to someone and they say that I had no choice, it makes me squirm. I'm so frustrated with myself. Why did I choose this way?"

"It sounds like you had a choice in the moment," I said, "but you had already made a choice before that. One around the story you told yourself, which was, 'This job is at risk and I could get fired.' And that would be a bad thing. Versus telling yourself, 'I'm a great worker. This guy's an ass. I don't need this job. I'm going to do my best, but I'm not going to violate my own boundaries.' So, that *was a choice in the story you told yourself before you made an actual physical choice."*

"Oy," Claire sighed. "*I feel so stupid. Why did I let my fear get the best of me? I know better too. I went to all the effort to set a boundary thirty days ahead of time. I thought I was really doing things with intent this time. Why did I choose this? Argh!*"

"Claire, the question isn't why. It's *when*," I said in my best scholarly voice.

That made her smile. Sometimes I forget to inject a little humor when I get deep into these serious conversations. We took a sip of our coffee and smiled at each other.

We hugged and parted ways, that final question was still lingering in the air.

"When?"

I don't think Claire fully understood what I meant.

It was driving me crazy. When had Claire made a choice to believe this way? And it was a choice. One that happens when our guard is down, and we aren't paying attention. The kind that latches onto our insides and, by becoming a life-sucking parasite, we become their new home.

What could have been the impetus? Did Claire's mom say something a certain way when she was a kid? Did some jerk in high school do something to embarrass the hell out of her? Something pierced her soul deep enough that it triggered her to give up her choice. To give up her power to believe. Whatever happened, her interpretation got locked in as the truth that is part of the core to her story.

Why she did it doesn't matter. She gave her power away. Now she finds herself ten years later, missing out on Christmas with her father because she believed that some job, which wasn't that important, had to take precedence over everything else in her life.

Ouch! Another papercut.

--- -- - *A Shift* - -- ---

When was the last time you paid attention?

I mean truly paid attention. To the world. Your spouse. Your friends. Your boss. Focused on and listening. Connecting to the eyes, heart, and energy of the people and things around you. Seeing them for not only what they seem like from your immediate perspective but also from their perspective and others. Immersing yourself such that your senses are saturated from the outpouring of all that is around you; as if you were sitting in the middle of a sphere with sounds, smells, and other sensations hurling themselves at you from every direction, all at once.

Your mind quiet. Your eyes not to be trusted.

You can taste the sounds. The texture their resonance creates as it floats through the air.

The smell of emotions. Their thickness billowing all around you.

The tingle that starts in your toes, arcs through your arches, shivers up your legs, hardens your nipples, and exits through the peach fuzz-like hairs that encircle the exterior of your ears.

That.

[PAUSE and let yourself sit with whatever thoughts you currently have for the next 60 seconds.]

I would guess this isn't how most of us spend our days. Let alone five minutes a day. It can be scary, if we're honest with ourselves—all those sensations, the ones we work so hard to shut ourselves off from, flooding in and taking over our minds.

"But I don't shut myself off from those feelings," I can just hear you saying to yourself right now.

Oh really?

"Well at least not on purpose. I mean, no one likes to be overloaded by these types of feelings, but I definitely have them. I let them in. Multiple times a day," you say.

It's hard to deny that we are scared shitless of our feelings and of our thoughts. That we will do anything possible to NOT feel them. Not to taste or hear them, as the sounds lure us, beckoning us to pay attention.

"*Well, I'm not scared*," says your all-powerful little man of an ego.

OK then, great.

Follow me, please.

I have found that the best way to test this out is through a little coherence exercise. You just told me you aren't scared, so have a little faith and play along. This is also my favorite way to get present quickly or to start a deep-dive conversation with others, especially one that asks for vulnerability.

Three-Minute Dive:

1. Place your hand over your heart, close your eyes, and take three extra deep breaths, pushing all the air out quickly on the out-breath.

2. With your head bowed, move into 5 seconds in, 5 seconds out circular breathing pattern with no pause at the top or bottom of the breath. Do this 18 times.

3. During this 3 minutes breathing exercise, bring to mind the last time you truly felt joy. An experience of happiness, soulful fulfillment, or utter peace. Bring the energy of that moment into your heart. Let the feeling slowly melt, dripping down your arms, onto your thighs, and trickling out through your toes.

4. Before you open your eyes, send gratitude to three people. Now send it to yourself.

5. Smile!
----

find more rituals at: www.3xBold.com

Did you make it?
Good. I figured you would.

How do you feel? Actually, I hate this question, don't answer it.

What do you feel?

Where do you feel it?

Did some of the tension you had stored in your shoulders, neck, or legs get released?

Are you just a wee bit more at ease?

Do you find yourself slightly more curious?

Whatever you are feeling, it's doubtful that it's worse than before we did this centering exercise. My challenge to you is to play. Experiment. If these last three minutes sparked even the slightest shift in energy, perception, anxiety…anything, then I encourage you to make it your own.

It can even be gamified.
How quickly can you change your level of presence?
How fast can you find a shift?

There's an age-old story of two salesmen who went to Africa in the early 1900s. They were sent down to determine if there was any opportunity for selling shoes.

After spending a week tromping through cities, villages, and the countryside, they both looked at each other. Nodding yes in agreement, they turned to their guide and asked him to take them to the closest train station.

The guide was shocked as the two gentlemen still had one week left on their tour. He told them stories of other villages in remote parts of the country and about the amazing wildlife they had yet to see and experience. But it was to no avail, as they had seen enough.

Arriving at the closest train station, which also had a Western Union office in it, they both wrote telegrams back to their head office in Manchester.

Salesman 1: "Situation hopeless. Stop. Nobody here wears shoes."

Salesman 2: "Glorious opportunity. They don't have any shoes yet."

It's important to remember that it's all about choice, particularly the small ones. Are we going to stay stuck and allow another layer of grime to build up on our skin? Spinning the same stories from the same perspective that become the blue shade of glasses we see the world through? Or are we going to choose to embrace a shift? How about simply making an effort, regardless of the outcome, shift or no shift?

We no longer have to ignore our choice here.

--- -- - Conscious Decisions - -- ---

Habits matter. Especially the ones where you exercise your God-given right to choose. Creating consistency is key. A daily awareness with a minute-by-minute cadence. Flexing the muscle of using our most powerful gift.

Choosing choice. Making it a conscious decision.
Not one that we relegate to our automatic programming.
And not one that we choose not to make.

In Tommy Baker's 2018 book, *The 1% Rule*, he proposes that the fastest and most consistent way to reach a goal or make progress is in baby steps. Specifically, his formula urges us to create a habit of trying to improve by a minuscule amount of 1% per day. It's an interesting concept and tallies some impressive results. If we apply the 1% Rule to how we make choices, then we typically see one of the following three outcomes.

Unconscious Choice
This is when we push the choice down to our reptilian brain, the brain stem, where all of our fight-or-flight decisions are made from. It's the core of our automatic response network. This part of our brain doesn't want our input, wouldn't listen to it anyways, and responds in black-and-white ways that are meant to keep us from dying.

When we ignore the agency we have over choosing differently every time an experience we're actively part of needs us to choose, then it reverts to what we've chosen in the past. In essence, it's a cop-out. The lazy choice. It's why so many of us feel like we are constantly spinning in circles, unable to gain traction in life.

Nothing good and no forward movement comes from doing the same things, over and over, and miraculously expecting different results. According to Einstein, that's called insanity. Yet too often this is our go-to choice. Easy. Simple. Effective. Bland. Stale. Pathetic.

When we embrace apathy, the outcome is that nothing changes. Showing up without any additional effort gets us 100% of the results we previously got. No more, no less. Over the course of a year, we get:

$1.00^{365} = 1.00$

It's like having our entire life savings in a noninterest-bearing checking account. It's safe but we miss out on the possibility of any upside.

<u>No Choice</u>
Whether we ignore, forget, are scared, or are simply indecisive, the choice of no choice is a very powerful choice. It's worse than you could ever imagine. The downside that our lack of choice can expose us to is almost unfathomable.

A measly 1% drop in effort has deleterious effects.

$0.99^{365} = 0.03$

Maybe this doesn't hit home hard enough for you. Let's stick with the bank account analogy. If you had $100 in your savings account, at the end of one year you would only have $3. Ouch!

Conscious Choice
Your present. Plugged in. Showing up in life with curiosity and empathy. You know that the choice is yours to make, and you've brought excitement and creative abandon with you. They're more than your cheerleaders, they're your teammates. Your best friends from childhood who you know have your back no matter what. They won't let you fail.

The mind-blowing part is that the habits and rituals we create here have an insane return on investment. Just 1% additional effort each day results in a 38% increase after one year.

$1.01^{365} = 137.8$

I don't know about you, but if I knew, and I do now, that my skill set, relationships, income, and happiness could steadily increase this dramatically, with such a small amount of effort, then what in the heck are we waiting for?

The bottom line is, when we improve something by one percent every day for a year, we make it 37% better by the end of the year. Alternatively, if we put in one

percent less effort every day for a year, we make it 97% worse.

Let's not pretend or kid ourselves here. Even with all of this knowledge, forward movement is tough. It can feel downright impossible, like trudging through knee-deep mud that keeps getting thicker and deeper by the moment. It takes effort to swing our legs through the mud, plant our feet, and regain balance. We turn our heads, look back, and then work on the other side. Same effort. Same struggle. Boom. Both feet are now even. We are one step ahead.

Damn! This 1% shit is hard! Yep, it's work. Intentional work.

No one is stopping us from sitting down. Let's take a break. We deserve it! The cool thickness of the mud is almost like a hug, and applying just the right amount of pressure to create the feeling of being held. Supported. It has our back, literally! Slowly, the mud fully encapsulates us, pulling us under. Better take a deep breath. Gasping. Choking. Oh, nooooo…

That's the easy choice. Or no choice. But definitely the lazy choice. And now we're stuck. Unable to move.

What if instead, we sought intent? No, demanded it? George Bernard Shaw understood this when he said, *"Life isn't about finding yourself. Life is about creating yourself."*

What if we became the jockey of our life? Sliding into the saddle and running our fingers through the sweaty mane of our race-ready thoroughbred. Locking our feet into the stirrups, pushing our heels down, and gripping tightly with our thighs. Feeling the tension build as we wait with bated breath behind the starting stalls. It's the calm before the storm.

This is intent.

As the bells ring and the gates slide open, we're ready. Facing forward, connected with the horse, we are as one. We meld with the animal under us and allow our trust to unfold completely. As we round the track, everything is in sync. Horse to rider, rider to horse. Every rise. Every fall. Winning is no longer the intention because we aren't competing to win. We're co-creating this experience, this journey with another being, and both of us are giving it our all. Our best.

And there's the intention.

Whatever comes out of this can be nothing but pure joy. We gave it our all. What a thrill! We left everything we had all out on the track. Satisfaction, fulfillment, and gratitude wash over us in waves of ecstasy. We chose. Consciously. We plant the seeds of intent and lean into full intentionality.

This is what winning really is.
This is how we create.

Stepping into the power of choice.
And owning our gift.

--- -- - *The Power of Intent* - -- ---

The door clicked as the handle rolled off my fingertips. Shut, but not latched. My hands full with wallet, keys, phone, and notebook, I invoked a little hip-swing move I have been working on over the years. Pivoting 90 degrees to the left and simultaneously lifting my right heel, I swung my backside toward the doorjamb. With perfect accuracy, my right butt cheek caught the edge of the door. I applied the perfect amount of pressure to avoid causing a dent anywhere. The door clicked again. This time, the deeper, more solid sound meant the car could now be locked, confirmed with a chirp from the key fob. Winning!

Strolling away and shifting my gaze in front of me, a blue Ford pickup turned into the parking lot, causing me to come to an abrupt halt. It was my friend Drew. My coffee date. This was not his normal car, though. I wondered if he got something new.

Distractions. Too many of them. Especially before caffeine.

The dryness in my mouth brought me back to why I was excited at the moment. Through the double pain glass doors, I could see my order, a grande nitro cold brew with a splash of oat milk, was waiting for me at the counter.

That wasn't why I showed up here today, though. Bringing my focus back to where I stood, I decided to wait and walk in with my friend. We shook hands, smiled, and warmly greeted each other, aka a man hug. Our friendship was born roughly five years earlier when we met at a business mastermind group. From day one, we have been trusted confidants and have always found immense value in the unique perspective of the other person. I'm immediately reminded why I love this guy!

We quickly got lost in conversation and I had to ask for a brief pause as I grabbed my coffee from inside. It was a cool winter day in Phoenix, so we zipped up our coats, walked across the street, and found a seat in the plush lobby of a shared office space building on the riverwalk. This was our monthly ritual, and we had the place to ourselves today. The sun was streaming in through the 30-foot-tall front windows, reflecting off of Tempe Town Lake, and dancing across the back of the crushed velvet chair next to me.

Drew kicked the conversation off and said, *"Last weekend my wife and I celebrated our 14th anniversary."*

"Oh boy, that's significant," I gushed. *"Exciting. I can tell you are happy from the smile on your face. You've always been so intentional. So present. I've always admired how you show up for your family. You may not know this, but I'm always taking a lot of mental notes when we get time together."*

(He creased his lips, almost closed his eyes, and grabbed his heart in a gesture of appreciation.)

"*Yeah,*" Drew went on. "*We were laughing and thinking, what's our life going to look like in another fourteen years? No kids in the house. No more hustle and bustle of the shuffle.*"

Laughing, I said, "*Ha, you should write that down. That's poetic, my friend.*"

"*I couldn't have planned that if I wanted to. Writing is not something I'm known for, to say the least,*" he retorted.

We paused to let the moment sink in, and 30 seconds slipped by before we knew it. I took a long breath in through my nose and continued, "*Something I realize as I reflect back on those years in my own marriage is, where did the time go? I mean, it all went so fast. And as I think about intention, it's glaringly evident that intentionality is something I rarely, if ever brought to my marriage and family. Now, I sure did think that I was being intentional, but, in retrospect, I definitely was not.*"

"*I think,*" chimed Drew, "*that goes for most of us. On most topics. We are all always just doing our best even when we're oblivious to what is really going on.*"

"Have you ever thought much about the intent to be intentional? Does that even make sense to you?" I wondered.

"I'm not sure. I think I hear what you are saying."

"Drew, I know that one of the big reasons you have been able to thrive in your marriage, for the last fourteen years, has been carving out time for you and your wife to have as a couple. To play. To love. To hold each other. When you make time for her and treat it as sacred, that is intentionality.

The question becomes, how do you get yourself prepared for these moments of intentionality? Are you driving across town from an appointment that has you arriving on time yet frazzled? Or are you preparing your day in a way that you get home two hours early, so you can take a quick shower, change, turn your phone on 'do not disturb,' do a 5-minute breathing exercise and a 10-minute meditation or prayer? I know you prefer to pray. You prioritize time to do what you need to do in order to show up fully present. That is how I would describe having intent to be intentional."

"That's a really interesting way to think about things, Brent. And no, I don't think I nor many others do this very well or often enough."

"I know that for most of my life, I haven't shown up like this," came my reply. *"It might have taken me a decade or two, but I get it now. It's simply amazing. That something so simple can provide such exponential improvement to a practice that is already so special. Intentionality is a gift on*

its own, and the addition of intent serves only to supercharge this gift.

"In simple language, intentionality means we are doing something with deliberate focus, usually to the betterment of someone other than ourselves, though not always. Bringing intent to the front end of this process really is us being uber-present. Living fully in the here and now.

"When we combine presence with intentionality, there's nothing more human. This is what connection at the deepest level looks and feels like."

"Absolutely," Drew agreed. *"The cool part is that we can practice this on the little things. The daily interactions we have with family, friends, or coworkers. In fact, I'm going to go do this for my next meeting. Instead of rushing in, all frantic and trying to clear my brain of what happened in the previous meeting, I'm going to take a couple of minutes. Catch my breath and slow down. Find presence and gratitude for the person I'm going to spend the next 60 minutes with."*

"Funny enough, Drew, one of my really close friends modeled this perfectly. She wanted to create a space of intentionality, and in her wisdom, she knew that a little front-end intent was direly needed in order for us to get the most out of our newly budding friendship. Here's how she set the stage:

'Divorce sucks. I've been there. You go to some dark places. And at the risk of crossing a major line here, you are anything but unlovable. I loved you instantly. Your warmth and vulnerability are beacons that shine brightly, and anyone should be lucky enough to bask in them with you. Please don't take this the wrong way. I'm a very happily married, loyal wife and not looking for anything more than for another human (you) to recognize just how delightful you are. You are so much more than enough. Know you are loved.'"

"Wow!" Drew shook his head as the words came out. "I am blown away. That gave me the chills. I've never had someone show up like this, Brent. Especially not out of the gate!"

"I know, right? Thanks to her taking a risk, finding intent, and setting the stage, it pays tribute to why we have such a deep and amazing friendship today. Maybe this makes it sound too easy. I mean, why do we so often think we don't have an extra three minutes to find intent for our next move, next interaction, or for what we intentionally desire to create in life?

I laugh at the silly thoughts that stream through my head. I was just thinking that it's no different than us preparing to make a turn when we are driving. In fact, it's so important that there's actually a law around it. What is it, something like 500-feet minimum before you turn, you must put on your turn signal? And using turn signals ends up being the intent part of the equation. We get lazy, though, and zoom in and out of traffic, making last-minute decisions and not using our turn signals. And what happens?"

"We frustrate other drivers at best and could cause a serious accident at worst," Drew added. *"Yet we don't apply this logic to life. What if the exponential gain works in the other direction? What if instead of intent making intentionality 300% better, the lack of intent makes our intentionality only 50%, or much less, of what it could have been? Could intent, or the lack thereof, be the proverbial double-edged sword of intentionality?"*

"Hmm, you are wise beyond your years my friend. I think you could be on to something, Drew."

"I can't take any credit here. In fact, it's so interesting as I reflect on how it ties in perfectly with my devotional from this morning. I was working in the Barclay's Daily Study Bible *and it was contemplating the meaning behind Matthew 22:11-14. The lesson from this parable was:*

'Too often we go to God's house with no preparation at all; if every man and woman in our congregations came to church prepared to worship, after a little prayer, a little thought, and a little self-examination, then worship would be worship indeed—the worship in which and through which things happen in the souls of men and women and in the life of the Church and in the affairs of the world.'"

"Ah," I thought out loud. *"It seems to me that when we take the time to start with intent, we move from 'being' to*

'engaging' as we move into intentionality. Don't get me wrong, learning how to 'be' is such an amazing first step, as it shows presence.

Engagement is 'being' with action. It's presence with fortitude and stability."

Matthew 22:11-14
New International Version
11 "But when the king came in to see the guests, he noticed a man there who was not wearing wedding clothes.
12 He asked, 'How did you get in here without wedding clothes, friend?' The man was speechless.
13 "Then the king told the attendants, 'Tie him hand and foot, and throw him outside, into the darkness, where there will be weeping and gnashing of teeth.'
14 "For many are invited, but few are chosen."

PAPERCUTS

Chapter 5:
WHAT'S IN THE MIRROR

--- -- - *Reflections* - -- ---

Maybe it's you.
Maybe it's me.

"Huh, who? Me?" I imagine your internal voice choking on the thought of this.

Of course, it's you, I mean me. You know what I mean!

Let's leave it to the experts to settle this. According to Lauren Handel Zander, in her book *Maybe It's You*, "*The only thing in common with every last thing that isn't working in your life is you.*"

It seems that we are the common denominator in the equation of our life. Shiitake (as my mom used to say).

Getting uncomfortable with and taking an honest look at our own role in this delusion of the illusion is our next stop. We're at the point in our journey where we can no longer passively read and consume these ideas. It's time to let our guard down and get vulnerable.

Let's clear this up one last time. Whenever our internal voice pops in and says, *"Who me?"* Just remember that the answer is always *"yes."*

With that, I think we should start with something easy and light: Inner Peace. (Okay, okay. Maybe not so easy and light. Sarcasm is the spice of life when it's used properly, and we all know my affection toward spicy things.)

When was the last time you had peace in your life? This question came up in a conversation among friends recently. The answer from all eight of us was a unanimous never. NEVER!

There was, of course, a certain type of peace that we have each experienced at some point in our lives, but it was always fleeting, temporary, or just one of many adjectives used to describe a particular event. None of us knew what true peace was. Peace as a state of mind, a way of life, or simply stillness.

Sublime serenity.

Each of us reminisced about times in our lives when we found ourselves magically transported to these moments. For me it was at the end of a long and arduous hike, staring across a sea of 14,000-foot peaks amidst the troughs of windswept valleys. Others found it during an intense prayer or meditation session. One lady recanted the most vivid and beautiful dream that left us all with jaws hanging open and drool beginning to pool in our lower palate. Another couple had it wash over them in what they described as a tingling paralysis of euphoria during a concert they were attending.

Peaceful and beautiful moments without question, but not peace. Not a peace that is sustaining. A peace that only shows itself when we really know ourselves, trust ourselves, or love ourselves. Peace > peaceful.

"When we know ourselves?
Really?
I know myself," you rebut.

Do you?
Who the heck are you, at your core?
And what are we talking about when we say "ourselves"?
What is the "self"?

We have been blessed on this earthly journey with a body. Call it a meat suit, a windbag, a worldly avatar, spit and dust, an earthly vessel, a water satchel, the rib of Adam, or whatever brings a smile to your face. Our bodies need a driver, and the lucky winner is none other than our ego.

The ego manages our five senses and gives texture to our interaction with this world. The role it plays is nothing short of amazing. From keeping us safe, fed, oxygenated, and constantly seeking admiration (and coitus), the ego lives a busy life. It also enjoys all types of fuckery. And not the fun kind that happens when you're in college and let loose a little more than you probably should have. The ego is a master at playing these games on itself. To make matters worse, his default attributes are often being fearful, cocky, and selfish. Our egos can be the definition of a train wreck sometimes.

Full of doubt, questioning everything, and responding to fear in milliseconds, things can get wild and out of control quickly. *"But I'm only concerned for your safety,"* the ego pleads with you. Not that we believe this ploy, but the ego's a good salesman. He knows just what to say and what buttons to push. He might be trained as a first responder, but he's not a surgeon, a lawyer, or an accountant.

Stay in your lane, ego!

It's rare that we actually need his Johnny-on-the-spot skillset to protect us from danger. And yet we end up consciously giving over control, automatically relinquishing or simply conceding, usually because it's the easy and brainless thing to do. This part of ourselves, the ego, the small "s" self, is what we defer to in much of our daily life, including our decision-making and our rationale. The majority of those 60,000 thoughts flip through our brains every day. Yep, we let the ego deal with them as he pleases.

--- -- - *Corridor of Echoes* - -- ---

Then there's the secondary Self. The more elusive, calmer, wiser, and older sister. The part of us connected to something beyond our daily experience here on Earth. Often referred to as the capital 'S' Self. I believe most of us know she exists, that she's in there somewhere. We understand that she's a part of us, but how and why can be obfuscated. She's our tether to deeper and wider connections with other humans. Sometimes called the soul, our essence, the psyche, spirit, or pure love, she is our connection to the divine. To the afterlife, if one exists, and all other nonphysical _____ (fill in the blank). Whether you've experienced this in your dreams, during prayer, deep in meditation, or during another left-brain quieting event, we've all had an experience or two with her at some point.

It's the whisper, the echo, or more often the sensation you get when you find a moment of peace. A moment when we can quiet the ego and are able to listen for the small self. It's the gaps in the silence, not the silence itself, but the spaces in between. It's what many of us are scared of. Silence tends to be uncomfortable on its own, and yet reading between the lines of silence, or better yet, listening in between the lines of silence, is where we will find the essence and sparks of magic. It's where higher knowledge, a deeper sense of self, and connection to the infinite lies.

The path there is not always easy or self-evident. Ever available and sitting in silence, it waits patiently for us to find our way. The path to get there, wherever that is, has no common name or route. Each of us, whether we've found it yet or not, understands it as something different. For me, it's The Corridor of Echoes.

I open the door. There's darkness. I can feel the depth pulsating in slow waves from afar. As I step into this long hallway of a room, my ears perk up. Off in some distant corner, I can hear that it's story time. Just like being in kindergarten, right before nap time, only it's our ego, reading from the story of our life. His version of it. Reverberating. Calling me back, beckoning me to retreat. As I push deeper, further into the depths, the echoes begin to fade. Reaching the most remote part of this seemingly never-ending abyss, I stumble upon my truth. My spirit. My Self. This is where I get an embrace of what feels like a warm hug.

Welcome to who you really are, Brent Perkins. You're not a VP of Whatever, not a father, not a lover, not a Captain of Industry, or a goal-scoring athlete superstar. Just you. Your Self. My Self.

Direct access can be tricky. Traversing this path is scary at times, rarely straightforward, and always evasive. And when we can't access her through this more direct route, which often ends up being through prayer, meditation, or dream states, all is not lost. She's still signaling and guiding us. She still has our back, acting as our guardian (angel?).

When we pretend or conveniently forget that she doesn't exist, or we numb access to her through one of our favorite techniques, like being too busy or having too much wine, she's still there, waiting patiently for us. The small self, the ego, has spent so many years creating this external image of who we are that distractions are second nature. When we have things to do, places to go, and people to meet with, we pretend like these distractions are meaningful and fulfilling. Oh, and super important, of course.

"Someone needs me," you say with pride. *"I can't say no. They can't make it without my help."* The feeling of being needed in some way for something is one of the ego's greatest tricks. Not much else makes us feel special and important quite like the made-up story that we are desperately needed. As if the world wouldn't be able to move forward without our grand expertise or magical touch. We let it define us, to get rooted into our deepest nooks, through the bone, and down into the marrow. The hooks are set. A false image of who we aren't, yet think we are, often locks us out of our own personal corridor of echoes, preventing us from tapping into the higher, wiser, and eternal part of ourSelves.

Don't believe the man on the soapbox doing a dance and waving his arms. He's crazy looking and distracting for a reason. He can't afford to have you not pay attention to him and you can't afford to be distracted by him.

You need you. First and foremost.

You need your Self.

"And as much as I'd like to
Believe there's a truth
About our illusion, well
I've come to conclude
There's just nothing beyond it
The mind can perceive
Except for the pictures in
The space in between"
>   - **Jan Blomqvist**, "The Space in Between"

--- -- - *Liar Liar* - -- ---

In the poem at the end of chapter 2, *Requiem*, we were challenged with a question. Who's at the wheel? The question here is not whether it's you or not. Hopefully, at this point in our journey, we agree that we are the ones making our choices, or not making them, which we know is still a choice. The real meat of this question is about self or Self. Which part of you is driving? Who's in control?

Too often, the self, the ego, takes over and we don't even know it. He is so stinking good at getting his way and pushing his way in, under the guise of protecting us, that we don't even see him slip past us into the driver's seat. Simultaneously barking commands and pulling levers on our choice-making master console. This is definitely not his first day on the job.

Exposing his secrets, lies, and the web he spins to keep us in a protective cocoon is our life's mission. Understanding the intent he has, which, in his own way, is only out of love. A misguided love, but love nonetheless, which makes our mission even more manageable. We are not here to hate on the ego. To tell it to "Bugger off." To kick it and tell it never to return. We *need* our ego. We couldn't survive in human form without him. But that doesn't mean we need to pander to his antics. Especially not the ones that don't provide us with any tangible value. Which, for the record, is a large majority of them.

Understanding where the ego's job starts and stops is ultimately what we're seeking here. I'll give two examples, one political and one sports based.

In the theater of politics (at least in the United States), the ego, the self, is like the President. He lives and thrives on public attention. He is the figurehead that, on the surface, seems like he has all the power. He is constantly shaking hands, kissing babies, issuing orders, and flying around, showing and telling everyone how important he is. Everyone knows who he is, and we are, mostly, all scared of him in some way or another. What he says goes, at least in theory.

At the President's disposal is an advisory board called the Cabinet, which consists of 15 members who each bring unique viewpoints, experience, and wisdom to the table. A tribe of mentors, so to speak, to lend guidance when it's needed. The Cabinet shares many similarities with our higher Self. Like the Cabinet, the Self is there any time we call upon it, and silent when we don't want to listen or when we believe we have it all figured out on our own. It seems like a no-brainer for the President to tap into the deep wisdom that this council of experts offers, yet it happens rarely. The same holds true in our lives. Invaluable knowledge and wisdom with a connection to divinity are only a short inner journey away.

The game of baseball serves as an alternatively useful metaphor, only with a slight twist. When a team is playing defense, there are nine players on the field. There's a catcher, a pitcher, four players in the infield, and three players in the outfield. The ego, or self, is the pitcher. The Self is made of all the other players, those in the infield and the outfield, as well as the catcher. Life is always whoever's at bat.

The ego (the pitcher) is the one facing down and, ultimately, interacting with life (the batter). He ultimately decides whether to listen to the signals he is getting from the catcher. Who, uniquely out of all the other players on the field, has a vantage point that allows Her (the Self) to see the entire landscape of the game. Yet the ego has a choice. He can choose to throw a pitch that he deems appropriate and the best fit, or he can listen to the advice of the catcher, who is also getting signals from all the other players.

It's always about choice. The ego often decides that he's the expert and will pitch a fastball when the Self, being present, right behind the batter, has noticed that a slow curveball would be best served. The ego doesn't have the same perspective, patience, or humbleness that the Self does, so this goes unnoticed. Such is life.

There's so much we can't see, don't know, or will never understand. Pretending anything different is nothing other than a lie. A false precept. Purposeful manipulation.

Brent: "*You said to me, 'If my clients or my patients could only come to me with the understanding of the power of choice you are advocating for, it would make my job much easier. I could dive straight into the work to help pull them out of it.'*"

Jonas: "*Another way to put it is the story, the delusion as you call it, is the lies we tell ourselves without realizing we're lying. When life just happens to my clients and they come to me realizing they're lying to themselves and that they want to learn, then it's easier. Often, it's a dance where I have to reveal their lie, and the way they've lied to themselves in a compassionate way and then introduce another way for them to see it. An honest way. Seeing this honesty can be very painful and being able to breathe through that pain, whatever it is, sadness, guilt, or anger, then, and only then, after they've been resolved in that emotion, can they be in a state of being able to accept honesty. It's at this point that they often have an experience where they just feel like this is the next thing they should do, as guided from within. Then there is an inspiration or* *an insight of, "Oh man, is this what it's like? Could it be this way?" And then I just confirm to them that, yes, this is how it can be and feel.*

There is the conscious part of the ego and the unconscious part of the ego. Within there, we have defense mechanisms that have been developed over millions of years to play a role in protecting ourselves from pain and danger. This becomes a way to talk down from your mind, understanding how the ego deploys all the defense mechanisms it has access to. How it plays soccer or baseball, basically, the "game of the ego" so that one doesn't get caught up in or catch onto what's really going on. Only then can one experience more. My takeaway is that instead of thinking thoughts, one is feeling one's thoughts or receiving thoughts more often. This is a way to think deeper and not get caught up in the surface thinking, which is where we tend to get negatively delusional and trick ourselves."

It's up to us to find an acute awareness of how the self operates and why he does what he does. Once we find ourselves noticing the lies, the tricks, and the slippery nature of his standard mode of operation, we can begin to respond differently. We can reclaim our voice and climb back into the driver's seat.

We always have the final say. The final choice.

For me, the memory that always gets triggered is the one when I'm out for a special meal with friends. Usually, this is a once-a-year event at a swanky joint. What always happens at the end of the evening? Kate won't stop talking, John looks like he shouldn't have had that last glass of wine, and I'm rubbing my belly and groaning that I ate too much.

The waiter comes out, *"Who wants dessert?"*

Oh boy. Seriously?

Yes (emphatically)!

"What are the options?" The words come out of my mouth a little too quickly.

This is what I often think about and feel like when I am given the final choice. On many occasions, I just sit quietly and wait. I wonder who else is interested in dessert. Not even slightly hungry myself, I let someone else make the decision. I know that a little bit would taste delicious, but eating sugar is the last thing I need. Temporary pleasure wins again! Cue the self-loathing and regret.

I am regularly left wondering: why is it so difficult to listen to our body and the Self to make the highest and best decisions for ourselves?

--- -- - *Comfortably Fearful* - -- ---

Every Wednesday morning my dad and I play cards, cribbage specifically, for an hour. This isn't some lifelong tradition or family pastime. We picked the habit up as his mobility and my schedule both started to deteriorate. It brings us together for coffee, storytelling, and a little friendly competition.

He tries hard to be patient, not give his opinion, and listen even though none of these things come naturally to him. He means well, though, as we all do. I have come to believe that we are all doing our best all the time. Sure, we get lazy and slip, but it's rarely intentional. We're all just trying to survive, live our best life, and hopefully find happiness and peace along the way.

Stirring the sugar into his coffee with his right hand, and holding his cards in his left, he was waxing on about divorce, second marriages, kids, grandkids, jobs, and social security benefits. It is not uncommon for our conversations to veer off on a tangent. With a little coaxing, his thoughts and ideas finally coalesced around the concept of "comfort zones."

"*When you are a kid,*" he started, "*you develop a comfort zone. I guess it's influenced by your parents, other family members, friends, school, and other things in life. My comfort zone was fairly large, due in large part to me not being the shy type. And being young, it's really easy to step outside of your comfort zone. Whether that be to make new friends, get into a romantic relationship, or at work. I know that there are lots of jobs I held that I would never do today. The same goes for friends I've had and women I've dated.*

The older one gets, the more this tightens up. Stepping outside of your zone gets harder and more uncomfortable. I guess it's because we all hate change. No one wants to do things differently or is less willing to when they get to be my age. It's another reason why we get to be so stubborn as our birthdays stack up.

It's also why my current wife and I get along so well. She and I share similarities in our respective comfort zones. We both like to do the same things and don't like to move outside of this zone anymore. Your mom and I really never had much in common and our comfort zones didn't overlap. She had..."

I had to stop my dad at this point. I love him but he can drive me nuts.

"Can I offer you an alternative viewpoint, Dad?" I asked, taking my time to get this sentence out of my mouth.

"Sure thing," he blurted before I could finish the last sentence with, *"Dad."*

"What if your idea of a comfort zone is really a fear zone? A zone of protection that keeps out all the things that might expose us or our ego for what it really is. What if it is

nothing more than a fake exterior to make sure we could never be vulnerable? Never be hurt. Never be wrong. Never be fully exposed?

Not just by other people, but by ourselves. To prevent us from feeling pain, for any reason.

This fear zone could be one of the ways that we attract new friends and lovers into our life. We intentionally let them know things about us, like: I like to watch movies, I like to karaoke, I like to watch football, I like wine, I like beer, I like camping, I'm a Democrat, etc.

What if it was our filter to see, as we got older, who we would spend time with, listen to, or let into our bubble?

Our comfort zone quickly digresses into the zone of enablement. You and I have talked before about how most days you watch 4+ hours of television, smoke a cigar, and drink some whiskey. These activities are all part of you living and being in your comfort zone. Your wife likes to do most of these things too and she doesn't care that you do the ones she doesn't do herself. She finds pleasure in enabling you.

This makes it easy and 'comfortable' for you."

"I never really thought of it that way, but yeah, could be."

"So, I'm curious, Dad. Who challenges you? Who is keeping you accountable and honest? Who's calling you on your shenanigans?"

"Well, no one. I don't want to change my ways. I certainly don't want anyone telling me what I can and can't do."

"I get that. Although, that's not exactly what I meant. You know the saying, 'Friends don't let friends drive drunk,' don't you?"

"Yes, of course."

"This slogan was designed to appeal to your heart and your intellect, served with a side of unspoken guilt. If we turn this around in our lives, the choices we make and what we ultimately decide to do, then we can see how it serves a similar purpose.

People in your life who care enough about you to pull you out of your bubble, or zone of comfort as you put it, instead of enabling it. The souls that are unfortunate enough to get sucked into a bad drug habit, like meth, what do they do? They surround themselves with other people that also do meth. They seek out others who party and numb out to life in a similar way to them.

Hunkering down behind the sandbag wall built around the outskirts of your fear zone is a way to avoid feeling like you are being judged."

It was two minutes past when he was scheduled to leave, so we hugged and he shuffled out my front door, leaving with a somber look on his face. Was I too honest? Too harsh? Too pushy?

My dad's got thick skin, but I wonder sometimes if he can handle where our conversations end up going. They're rarely surface level and fluffy. At least I try not to let them be on Wednesday mornings.

Fear zones are created by our egos to keep us safe and to prevent us from having to truly look inside. I believe they're one of the biggest ways that we get in our way to finding self-love and self-trust.

As we get older, churn through friends, lovers, and careers, we find other people who fall within our comfort zone and build them into our fortified barricade. The one encircling us and providing protection from the big bad buzz killer.

Cue the "easy button" commercial. Surrounding ourselves with people who accept all the things we do, advocate for and appreciate all the ways we hide and won't challenge us to be better, to go deeper, or to truly discover what or who we can be, is a choice. A very deliberate one.

Nothing about this is healthy or sustainable. So, why is this our default mode setting?

--- -- - *Wired This Way* - -- ---

Have you ever tried to keep a journal of your emotions or your feelings?

I did. My goal was to journal for one week, which would give me, I was told, incredible insight into how I functioned at my core. By lunchtime on day one I threw my hands up. In those couple of hours, I had filled an entire 8x11 sheet of paper and was spilling onto page two. The task at hand quickly felt overwhelming and I gave up. The lesson was not lost on me, though. We swing up, down, left and right all day long. Paying just a small amount of attention to it is exhausting! It's also confusing. What is an emotion, and how can I tell the difference when it becomes a feeling? This can bring overwhelm to overwhelm. Yikes!

Emotions and feelings are two different but connected aspects of the human experience. Many schools of thought exist here, as it's clear that we don't have definitive answers on exactly how feelings and emotions work. In general, it is accepted and understood that emotions are a physiological and psychological response to an external stimulus, such as a change in environment or a social setting. These stimuli can be anything from a sound to a smell to a touch or even a shift in a cultural norm. They are frequently referred to as a series of physiological changes that take place in the body and the mind in reaction to certain stimuli and are contingent upon the experiences of the individual.

Think back to the last scary movie you watched. One that had you at the edge of your seat, your legs tightening and your hand twitching, ready to grab a pillow or the person next to you. Odds are you were experiencing fear. Most of the time our emotions are accompanied by physical manifestations. Fear is no exception and is known to bring with it some wild physiological reactions such as an elevated heart rate, sweating, and trembling.

Feelings, on the other hand, refer to the conscious experience of our emotional state. These are how we interpret and name the experiences we have with our emotions. For instance, a person feeling scared would refer back to the underlying emotion of "fear" in their internal dialogue. Feelings are not only the verbal and mental labels we put on our emotional experiences, but they are also the way we express emotions to ourselves and others. All of which are impacted by society, previous experiences, and our personal beliefs.

(And, no, "fat" is not a feeling)

In short, emotions are the automatic and physiological reactions to certain events and feelings are the conscious experience (including additional physiological reactions) of emotions. Emotions are the raw data of our internal experience and feelings are the interpretation of that data.

This is GREAT NEWS!

We aren't destined to be ruled by our emotions. We can use them for what they were intended to be: a guide. An internal compass that is always at our disposal.

The body is our mansion. It is big and vast, with multiple rooms and an expansive garden. Mine has a sauna and a cold plunge too. Maybe yours has a 50-car subterranean garage or a spiral staircase that leads to a hidden glass chamber with 300 pairs of shoes. Maybe the dream includes an indoor pool filled with Skittles. We're not here to judge. Your body is yours and how you build out that mansion, both externally and internally, is completely up to you.

My guess is that we would all agree on the importance of protecting our mansion and those in it. At a minimum, there would be a security system with the windows and doors wired for alert. Oh, you're the type who wants a panic room with a full-on mission control center, where you can monitor your property and your belongings and call for help as needed? Sounds reasonable to me. After all, your things were hard-earned, precious, and full of memories, many of them irreplaceable.

Brent: *"Too often we use the filter of our brain, our intellect, to see if something sounds wise or true. Yet, we rarely use the filter of our body."*

Jonas: *"And how it's felt in the body, according to Damasio's research on somatic markers, are the older (reptilian) parts of the brain are assessing what they hear, compared to everything else it knows and it resonates as truth. It brings that truth through in the form of a delusion, which we then feel as truth.*

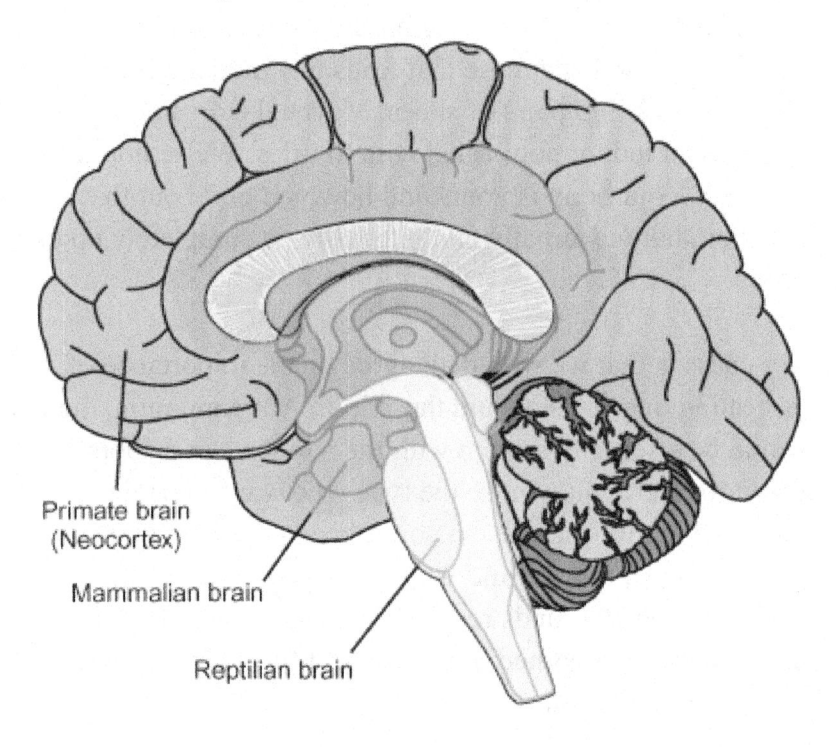

www.sciencedirect.com/topics/medicine-and-dentistry/triune-brain

"In simple terms, we have the reptilian brain (brain stem), mammalian brain (limbic system), and primate/human brain (neocortex), all stacked up and working together. When we say something (human) and feel another thing (mammalian) and then do an even different thing

(reptilian), they don't resonate, and we feel it in incongruent emotions. There's a conflict. When you say something that's in line with how you feel down deep and with your actions or how you experience the world, then you feel that as truth."

Brent: *"Interesting. I've never heard it described in a way that you need to have the brain stem, the limbic system, and your prefrontal cortex all in alignment, because there are three stages that govern who we are as humans, in terms of brain development over the last several million years. They're each processing it slightly differently, and the resonance between them is what ties together this system, from our gut to our brain."*

Jonas: *"It's different when you think your thoughts in order to more define when you get stuck in your story, versus when you think about your feelings, and start to get more into the limbic system, versus when you feel your feelings or experience them in your body, then the thoughts are just like bubbles floating up. Some call it a felt sense. When we remain present, it is interesting to ask ourselves how do we feel or how are we experiencing this felt sense?*

"This is where psychology has a lot to learn to come up with new words because psychology is 'psyche,' which is basically how we mentally interact with the world. Psychology should consider changing its name if we want it to include the human experience. A medical doctor will always work with medicine so we can't expect a medical doctor to include working with exercise to heal a person.

Mostly because it's so hidden and unconscious, these words and what they define. Physiotherapists, on the other hand, don't spend their time thinking about thoughts and emotions, because they are taught to understand and treat the body and muscles. Now we want to describe the human experience, so we can move more freely and play with things like the brain stem (physiological and the body), limbic system (emotions and feelings), and cognitive level.

"In my experience, when I reflect back on my clients, they are so hungry to understand the full human experience and that's why they often go to psychologists, but the clients rarely feel like it helped, because they are too often relegated to explaining things from a cognitive perspective."

In the 1960s, Paul Ekman proposed a theory of six basic emotions that all other feelings and emotions tie back to. Given that emotions are extremely complex, and we don't have definitive scientific proof or universally accepted absolutes, these six are a comprehensive and useful construct for us to continue to build upon. Dr. Gloria Wilcox built out the following Feelings Wheel that provides for the feelings we often experience as associated with their core emotions. She added "Bad" as a 7th emotion. Debating the merits of six or seven core emotions is not relevant to our journey. Being able to understand the concept of what an emotion is, how it's triggered, what a corresponding feeling could be, and how the two synergize is our goal.

The Art of Self-Delusion

FEELINGS WHEEL:

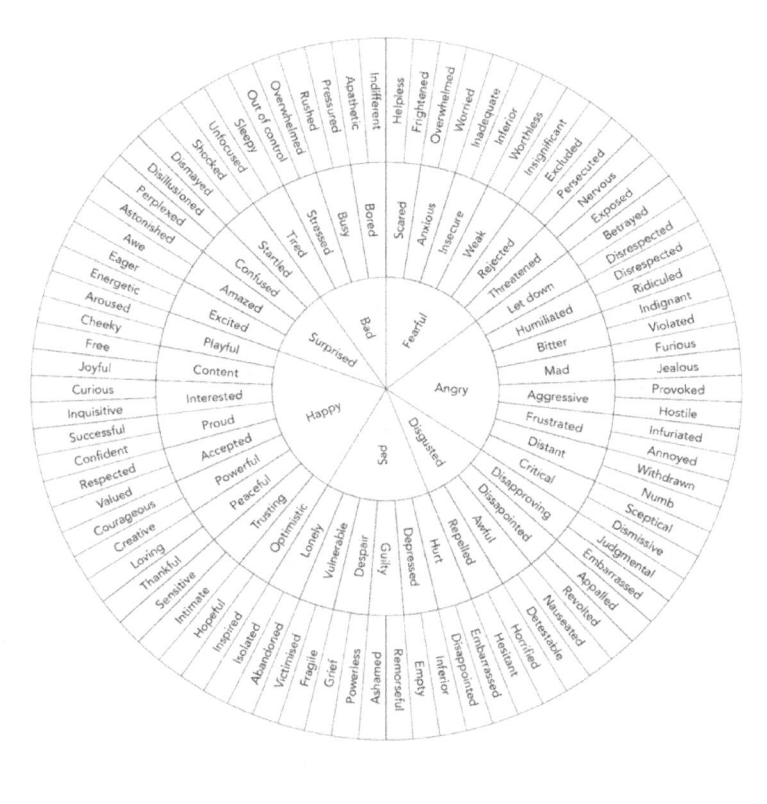

Originally created by Dr. Gloria Wilcox

I know it can get complicated and this is full of nuances, but "having" the emotion of sadness does not imply or guarantee that it must be felt in a certain way. I remember when my mom died, I was full of sadness, yet through my tears, there was joy, appreciation, and calmness. My emotion of sadness evoked feelings that we don't always associate with the underlying emotion. Yet, that's how my body was expressing sadness at that moment. At other times I've felt sadness as completely debilitating, like being unable to even get out of bed.

Our feelings are what we so often end up interacting with directly that it can be hard to categorize them as reflective and subjective. As we've seen here, feelings regularly cross over the categories of emotions, leaving us with no rhyme or reason as to their directive. This creates an unpredictable mosaic, leading to more confusion. The thread of understanding that weaves its way through our story gets lost. Our connection to why we are feeling this way gets severed. Then a new thought pops into our heads, followed by a new set of feelings.

Huh. Why do our feelings always feel so real? Like pure truth in the moments that we experience them?

--- -- - *The Feels* - -- ---

Feelings aren't facts.

Just because we *feel* less than does not mean that we <u>are</u> less than. From here, we can begin to understand that emotions happen to us and feelings are a choice.

Yung Pueblo, in his book *Lighter*, has a simple way to explain this. *"Most people walk the earth unaware that they are not seeing with their eyes. Instead, they are seeing with their emotions, and often these emotions are just echoes of their past hurts. Many fall into cycles of projection where they are taking their inner roughness and spewing it out into the world."*

I find it utterly fascinating that the same emotion can impact each of us so dramatically differently. The feelings evoked can't even be named as they span the entire spectrum of possibility. Yet this is where owning our **agency of choice** becomes so important. Because we have a direct influence here. I know it doesn't feel like it at the moment sometimes. Yet underneath it all, if we can stay present, choice is there. It's waiting patiently for directions from us. If we can only remember, especially in the tough moments, that our emotions are signals, not forceful commands. They are our body's way to let us know that something is stimulating us out of congruence. Emotions don't have the power to make us react, feel a certain way, or physically do anything. Emotions are never sitting in the driver's seat. This, whether we are ready to embrace it or not, is where we *always* have a choice.

There are occasions when an emotion hits us so hard and fast that it's only natural for us to get triggered. Those times when an automatic response is provoked, and deserving I might add. Yet we still have a choice; choice in how we react. Rage might be rightfully deserved yet the outward expression of it isn't mandatory. Nor must we choose or allow ourselves to be cast as victims. Stepping into and owning our choice allows us to be deliberate with our response. To know and trust ourselves so deeply that we don't defer to our default programs, even in times of intense pain or perceived attacks.

The quickest way to make yourself feel horrible is to focus on "making" others feel good. On that note, what the heck is "good" (as if there's a universal definition here), and how can you make anyone do or feel anything?

You can't. Knock that shit off and unapologetically bring the focus back to you.

I was out hiking on a Wednesday afternoon when I ran into a group of three people approaching from the other direction. Trail running is a better description of the activity I was engaged in that day, and I was intently focused on setting a new personal record (PR) and brainstorming some ideas for this book. As I approached them, they flagged me down and had me come to a stop. Their question was, *"Is the parking lot in the direction you are coming from?"* Although I was beyond irked, I calmly said, *"Yes, it is,"* and started jogging again. As I pushed past them, trying to get back into my rhythm, I heard one of them say, *"Geez, that was rude."*

Normally, I would've ignored it and kept going. But I was curious. Remember, I wrote this book for me. These are my lessons. So, in the process, I have taught myself to be curious, ask lots of questions, and question all the answers.

I quickly slowed down and pivoted, clearly catching the group off guard. I said, *"Please accept my apology if I have offended you for some reason. I'm curious though, what about our interaction has you irritated?"*

One of the older ladies in the group stepped forward, *"You barely slowed down to answer our question and you were so short about it."*

My eyes closed and shuttered under the lids as my head did one of those little shakes in pure incredulity. I was shocked by what I was hearing. Then it quickly turned to curiosity. I let their perception of reality (or delusion of the illusion) pass through me. Not ignoring it but not letting it stick to me either.

With no intention of proving a point, I merely wanted to understand this experience from their perspective. To see and hear what this interaction with me was like for them. The other hiker went on to explain that, visiting from out-of-state, they were unsure of the path and were hoping for some reassurance from a local. Hiking was something they enjoyed, however, getting lost and stuck in the cold desert at night was not what they had hoped for.

They were oblivious to my story (they never asked, so I didn't tell it), and somehow, they missed the guidepost 50 feet from them, which stated that the parking lot was .20 miles in the direction they were already headed. There's also Google Maps. But what do I know?

I apologized again and wished them well on the rest of their vacation. I continued onward, but I no longer had the option to chase a new PR.

The really crazy thing here?
Most of the above story never happened. At least not outside of my head.

I was trail running and did run into this group of three hikers. They also stopped me and asked me where the parking lot was. I answered quickly and kept going. Here's where things went a little sideways in my story.

As I ran past one of the ladies, I *thought* she gave me an odd smirk. The smirk turned into a verbal "geez," and the rest is history. It was all my delusion. Made up. Fabricated. With the best of intentions to protect my ego's position and that how I handled the situation was very appropriate. This story ran circles in my head for the next ten minutes as I got farther and farther away from them. Details of our interaction started to materialize and slowly filled in all the gaps. The story that I finally claimed as my reality was complete and airtight.

Locked in as my truth, and, at the same time, completely false.

Yet it triggered a fear of a lack of self-worth, and I let that emotion stir up all kinds of feelings that, in hindsight, seemed silly. It was all very real for me at the time, though.

It would have been easy for me to have recanted a version to my friends in a victimized fashion. Allowing the story and its corresponding physiological response to become part of my delusion. In fact, it would have even been fun to tell. Locals love to lament over stories about annoying snowbirds and other visitors that jam up our hiking trails. My emotions would have been justified, at least in my brain, and I could've further spun a story that would have let me wallow in my feelings for a few more days.

None of it would have served me, though.
Nothing here honors or protects my physical or mental health.

As I got in my car, I wondered, how often do we stop and ask ourselves this?
Do we ever consider the impact this has on us personally?

Anthony Robbins, the author of *Awaken the Giant Within*, has been researching and teaching these concepts since the early 1990s. His core takeaway messages align perfectly with what we have been discussing thus far:
- *Our emotions come from us. No one can give them to us or make us have them.*
- *We get to choose how we feel.*
- *Most of our beliefs come from random experiences and the circumstance of fate.*
- *Beliefs aren't absolute or fixed in time forever.*
- *We have the power to rewire our minds and choose to be who we want to be.*
- *Ultimate control of our internal world resides within us.*

There is so much power, right at our fingertips. Tony's entire life's work confirms that everything comes down to choice—which is what we have been talking about this entire time. We have:

Choice in how we react to our emotions (via feelings).
Choice to change our beliefs.
Choice to rewire our brains.
Choice over our story.

So much choice. It's overwhelming!
I'm starting to feel verklempt.
It hurts. My stomach. Arghh.
That pounding in my head.
My vision is going blurry.
Someone make it stop!

Oh, wait, that's me. Only I can choose to make it stop.
Shoot.
I didn't sign up for this!
Um, check, please!
Waiter! Waiter?

Get me the heck out of here.

--- -- - *Projections* - -- ---

Strolling across the trampled grass, pace quickening as the flashing lights loomed off in the ever-approaching distance. Patience has never been a virtue I've embraced, at least not for myself. Excitement and trepidation course through my legs and up through my chest. Ticket in hand and only four patrons ahead of me, the towering facade stares down from its perch. I shutter, one of those whole-body electrified twitch-filled shivers that rumbles down my spine.

The mouth that encircles the entrance is only a few steps away now. Red lips, inviting and beckoning patrons to enter. I stepped onto the rolling pink tongue that ushers one through the toothy smile and into the unknown.

Slow and deliberate
A step forward is taken
Then another. And one more
The dim light and odd refractions come into focus
It's all around me
Panic!
I'm all around me
Fear and illusion closing in
I keep running into myself
Where is the other Self when I need her?
Confusion and helplessness abound
A boyish yelp echoing all around
Energized by the fear
An over-caffeinated egoic self
White knuckling for control
It seems that only dread is on the menu here
Turning left, it's me
Stumbling backward, it's still me
Why can't I see the path?
So many obstacles
Defeat fills my lungs
It's hard to breath

Constricting
The inevitable closing in
Obstacles everywhere
Reflections that can't be real
My face, my fear, my panic, my truth
Why won't it stop?
Why won't they get out of my way?
I'm stuck
The only option is to shut down
If only they would stop

How often does life feel like this? Like we've lost control and there's nothing else we can do. A hall of mirrors showing us all our deficiencies. The tiniest of imperfections. Our best never being good enough, yet the effort we put forward is valiant. Heroic even.

But that's not the problem. No one's debating our effort.

Each of our stories is being written from expectations. The desire for control. Biased assumptions influencing our every move. When did we give away our power? The belief that the world is out to get us. Cowering like a victim, afraid and frozen. Unable or unwilling to see over the edge of the hole we've dug and crawled into.

For the record, it's a nice symmetrical hole. As far as hole digging goes, I give it a gold star. If for nothing else, the effort put forth was pretty epic.

— Take a 15-second pause. Then three deep breaths —

The Art of Self-Delusion

Can I ask why, if we have effort to give, it's being spent on digging a hole? A nice one, but still a hole?

I was asking myself this same question on my drive home the other day. It had been a rough afternoon. Life had swindled me when I wasn't looking, and it wasn't fair. I was drained and just needed to be done with the day. As I rounded the corner and got to the edge of the cul-de-sac that I live on, I got a "ding." The following story popped up on my social feed:

"No piece of art has ever emotionally affected me the way this robot arm piece has. It's programmed to try to contain the hydraulic fluid that's constantly leaking out and required to keep itself running...if too much escapes, it will die so it's desperately trying to pull it back to continue to fight for another day. Saddest part is they gave the robot the ability to do 'happy dances' for spectators while the spill was contained. When the project was first launched it danced around spending most of its time interacting with the crowd since it could quickly pull back the small spillage.

Many years later... (as you see it now in the video) it looks worn down and hopeless...Because the amount of leaked fluid became unmanageable as the spill grew over time, there now isn't enough time to dance as it only has enough time to try to keep itself alive. Living its last days in a never-ending cycle between sustaining life and simultaneously bleeding out... (Figuratively and literally as its hydraulic fluid looks like it's actual blood.)

Sun Yuan and Peng Yu's *Can't Help Myself* (2016–19) at the Venice Biennale in 2019. *LAURA CHIESA/PACIFIC PRESS/SIPA USA/AP*

The arm slowly came to a halt and died in 2019, but with a twist—the bot, called a kuka servo, actually runs off of electricity, not hydraulics, so it was working its entire life towards something it didn't even need, tricked by the system it was brought into."

https://www.instagram.com/kricked/

It caught me just at the right moment and struck a chord somewhere deep. As the tears welled up in my eyes, a sense of overwhelm shot through my chest. Could this story about a robot be a visual representation of what happens when we tell ourselves stories steeped in delusions, based on the illusion we are living in?

To set the record straight, the story above isn't universally true. But it doesn't matter. This story was created from an artistic perspective to convey what the author saw and felt when he experienced this piece of art. It's his interpretation. It's perfect and it's true. For him.

There is a fragility to our stories. The delusions that our fears stack on and gain their power from. The daily dance the robot was preoccupied with was imagined as necessary to keep itself alive, staving off death and the fear that surrounded it.

Projecting our fears out into the world and noticing that our environment reflects them back to us can be confusing and scary. We may believe that we're witnessing something external to ourselves, an outside force or experience that isn't ours. Yet we would be mistaken. What we are seeing, feeling, and hearing is simply a reflection of what we are projecting out into and onto the world around us.

If we don't like what is being echoed back, maybe we should be conscious of what we are putting out in the first place. After all, the idea that *it might be you* is false.

It is you.

It always has been and always will be.

Chapter 6:
ARCHING THE NEMESIS

The screen of my Garmin watch reflected back to me, in perfect black and white, that today I'd hiked 9.3 miles. That's over 68 miles in total as today was day five of our trek. Only two more days and about 25 miles left. What had I gotten myself into? The excitement that had built up and gotten me this far was turning into regret. There was one way in and now only one way out, and no, a helicopter wasn't one of my viable options.

The Wonderland Trail circumnavigates Mt. Rainier and is nothing short of a wonder. To this day, I haven't seen the diversity and quantity of beauty that I did during those seven days and 93 miles. It was epic.

Epically stupid. My legs hurt. My feet felt like they were going to fall off. I had sores on no less than seven of my toes. My back had shooting pains going in every direction. My stomach ached for real food. My brain wanted a full night's sleep. Every part of me was demanding something that I couldn't accommodate.

Through all of the discomfort, the beauty, tranquility, and grandiose nature of all that surrounded me shone through. I was feeling beyond blessed that I had the privilege of being immersed in all of life's best handiwork. It was all on display. Trees, flowers, waterfalls, glaciers, animal life, wild blueberries. It was endless.

I'm not a fan of overstimulation. Big crowds, crazy events, screaming kids, cackling grandmas, drunk sports fans—not my choice of where to spend my time or energy. If you're trying to keep me honest, then you're probably about to call me out on my spicy food addiction. Fair. Consuming every meal with too much spice is, of course, overstimulation, and also the reason I had to break this habit.

Being on the trail was the antithesis of overstimulation. Only it wasn't. In ways that I didn't even know existed, each of my five senses was being tickled like keys on a piano during a concerto. The smells, sounds, and scenery were intense. Coming at me from every direction, all at once and layered on top of each other. Pine, wet rock, moldy wood, fungi, birds, squirrels, bears, bees, waterfalls, rivers, streams, springs, glaciers melting, boulders tumbling, eagles soaring, whew! This was overstimulation in the most enthralling way. *"Hell yeah,"* I thought. *"Bring it on!"*

The reality of everything I was immersed in was not lost on me. I was doing something that less than 300 people a year earn the privilege to do. Yet, it was this line of thinking that brought on even more guilt. More pressure. How could I have come all this way, experienced beauty at this level, and still struggled to find purpose in it all?

For clarity, I started this journey with one goal. One thing to accomplish on top of and outside of the physical portion of the journey. The strenuous nature of these trips ends up shutting down the mental gymnastics that usually block access to the deep truth I am seeking. Finding a way to unlock the door and gain access to the answer was something that I have reliably experienced in the past. The last occasion that was particularly memorable occurred during a four-day trip to the Grand Canyon. We had an arduous hike starting at the North Rim, down to Thunder River, laterally to Tapeats Creek, down to the Colorado River, up to Deer Creek Falls and the plateau above it, and on out through Bill Hall. It was no joke, and it was hot. Like 110 degrees hot. Never before have I been so spent, arguably due to heat exhaustion. During the final trek out of Deer Creek, I spent the better part of four hours hiking on my own, contemplating life, my job, and my family and doing my damnedest to come up with a name for a product my company was hoping to launch in the next 90 days.

It took about 45 minutes that morning to get into the zone, a state of flow, as I trudged up the steep switchbacks. With my mind finally settled and the left side of my brain switched off, the creative and ruminating juices started to flood in. Epiphanies about life, my family, the spiritual path I was currently on, my career, and other aspects of life came shooting in like lightning bolts. At about the three-hour mark, right on schedule, the door swung open and I stepped across the sill. There, waiting for me, was the name of the product that had evaded me to date.

Solved! This was always such a cool feeling. Fully immersing myself in nature, sweat, exhaustion, and a walking meditation was a surefire way to get me into this state of pure being.

Why couldn't I get to the state of pure being on the Wonderland Trail? Where was my blockage?

--- -- - *Sweet Stinger* - -- ---

I kicked at some rocks and found myself sulking. Seriously? How could anybody sulk on this trail? Then I started kicking myself, piling on the guilt. The shame. The empty threats of abandonment. Ouch! I was cutting deep.

With my head hung low and a visibly evident apathy in my cadence, I shuffled on. I made my way through the volcanic rock field that lay in front of me, my heart feeling heavy in my chest. Not thirty minutes prior, my senses were overwhelmed and my excitement piqued as we (my hiking partner and I) carefully picked our way across the outer edge of a glacier. It was such a cool moment. The undulating dirt-capped snow patch was just the lower tip of the ice formation that extended another two thousand vertical feet up the mountain.

Feeling crushed by the heaviness of defeat, my goal appeared to be impossibly out of reach. Five days in and I had nothing. No epiphany. No breakthrough. No magical insight or right-brain swarm of creativity. I just wanted a simple, "Ah-ha!" What was wrong with me? Was I trying too hard? Was my goal too lofty?

I pouted and walked. My demeanor grew grumpier and more cynical with each step. It was all I could do to put one foot in front of the other. All motivation was drained from my body. The terrain became desolate, bare, and ugly. I just put my head down and closed my eyes.

As I stopped to catch my breath, my hands found their way to my hips and my head tilted back. A deep breath released through my nose and cleared out through my mouth.

"*Goddamnit!*" I yelled.

I felt like such a whiny little baby. Two more deep breaths and my head started to clear.

I walked in utter silence, physically and mentally, for the next ten minutes. The black volcanic rocks and crushed grayish-brown dirt path streamed by in an endless loop. Something caught my eye. A lavender hue visually trailed out of the corner of my right eye. I stopped and scanned the landscape around me. Swinging my head up, I noticed a patch of green shrubs about shin high. Dotted every so often was a cluster of blueish-purple tubed-shaped flowers.

Coming out of my trance-like slog, I was now transfixed on the shrubbery that dotted the path, growing out of the surrounding rock bed. Something in me shifted. I had, maybe for the first time, let the feelings of lack, failure, and frustration wash over me. Refraining from judging them, I let them pass through me, and I leaned in, feeling their power, their pain, their heaviness.

The incline of the trail increased more rapidly now, causing me to look even further ahead to see what challenges still lay ahead. To my surprise and awe, the shrubbery grew ever thicker, blanketing both sides of the trail. Their flowers, the Broadleaf Lupine, became the dominant color, with swaths of them swaying gently in the breeze that was playfully blowing from behind along the path I was on.

Another deep breath.

Pushing forward with a little more oomph, the trail continued to climb, cresting a ridge within a few minutes. At the top was a felled log and a Southern view that went on for what looked like hundreds of miles. Mountain top to mountain top, it was an endless sea of peaks and valleys. The snowy peak of Mount Adams was directly to the South. Mount St. Helens was South and off to the right from my vantage point. These two peaks, along with Mount Rainier, formed a trine in the middle of the Cascade Range. Breathtaking is the only way that I can begin to describe it.

I peeled off my pack and leaned it against the log. My knees creaked and cracked as I sat all the way back, my butt landing with a thud on the hard dirt. Using my pack to lean against, I closed my eyes, crossed my arms and legs, and caught my breath. It took a minute or two for my heart rate to slow down and my body to fully relax. As everything in my world sought to find stillness, a gentle hum floated toward me in waves. At first, I could not distinguish it from the tinnitus I've lived with for the last 20 years. Only this was a much lower pitch than I was used to having to tune out.

My eyes fluttered open, and the expansiveness of the view hit me in the chest. I was on top of the world! What a landscape. What an experience. And to think that I couldn't stop bitching about petty what-ifs just minutes ago.

My gaze swept down across the prairie that rolled under and out away from where I was perched. The same blueish-purple flowers flourished in epic quantities here. Thick, dense, and in constant motion. Squinting and leaning forward, I became acutely aware that the droning was actually buzzing and that the constant motion was thousands of bees. Flying around, doing their job, and unaware of my apparent invasion.

As I took it all in, I felt a flutter on my shin. Two bees had landed there, but something was off. They were locked onto each other. Oh, snap, they were in a mating dance! Right then, the male bee locked its hind legs onto the torso of the female, began playing with her antennae, and made thrusting movements with his abdomen. His endophallus extended and attempted penetration...ON MY LEG!

Yes, I captured it on video. Thank you, iPhone!

My hiking partner strolled up and sat down next to me. *"Hot damn, are those bees humping? On your leg?"* he said, laughing.

Widening my eyes, I pursed my lips and nodded yes.

What a moment. An unscriptable journey leading up to this point and how I got to this exact spot, with heavy emotions that spilled over into my reality through feelings of lack and disappointment. Yet here I was, on top of the world. Nature fully engulfed my body and bathed my soul in its mystery.

Something was missing or I was missing something. It tugged at me, but my mind was blank. Have you ever had one of those moments where everything felt amazing? You were lost in the present moment, and everything was at peace around you. Then it hits you. Uh oh. How did I forget?

I'm allergic to bees!

That was what happened to me that day on the Wonderland Trail as we rounded the Southeastern slope of Mount Rainier. I was lost in the expansive view, with two bees creating the next generation of larvae on my lower leg. Most troubling was the now audible buzz of thousands upon thousands of other bees pollinating all around me. What was I thinking?

Clearly, I wasn't. Yet a calmness washed over me. Even as reality settled into my body and logic began to take back over. I had no fear. For the first time that I can recall, I was at peace with, maybe at one with, these bees that encircled where I sat.

By now I would usually be freaking the heck out. With no EpiPen in my bag, I would be in serious trouble if something went wrong. Not smart, Brent. As I went to stand up, something felt like it was pushing me back down. A gentle voice inside said, "Relax. Sit and take in this moment. It was designed for you." Little did I know that this moment was also designed by me. But I'm jumping ahead of myself.

We both ate a protein bar and slowly gathered our tired bones and packs. Swinging the packs over our shoulders and clicking the belt into place, we pushed on to our next campsite. As we descended away from the highlight of the day, the entire episode was on a replay/rewind/replay loop at 5x speed. I knew what just happened was special, but I didn't understand why or how.

We quickly dropped down into a valley where the sounds of a nearby waterfall came into focus. The Wonderland Trail continued to provide wonder around every turn.

That was when it hit me, or, as I prefer to think about it, hugged me.

I AM JUST LIKE A BEE!
I CAN STING or I CAN POLLINATE.
THIS IS MY CHOICE.

Goosebumps overcame my body in a head-to-toe wave. Here was the epiphany I had been seeking. Waiting for. Bitching about. I had stepped into a state of pure being. Finally!

As I reflected back on my journey that day, it dawned on me that we are all so powerful. That choice is always at our disposal and the implications of how we wield it can be intensely creative or unnecessarily destructive. The sea of purple flowers that transformed the black volcanic rock into a carpet of transfixing beauty wouldn't exist without the bees. And even though the bees held the power to sting, they chose to co-create through pollination.

I knew, right then and there, that I was a stinger. It's what I chose, what I still choose, as my go-to weapon. Reacting to the world around me in ways to prove my knowledge, power, and self-worth.

--- -- - *Anaphylaxis* - -- ---

This was seven years ago now. As I write this, it is only in the last six months that I feel I fully get this. That I live my life in a way where stinging isn't even on the menu anymore. Replaced, instead, by all the ways I can pollinate.

The fear I carried around protecting my modus operandi of stinging manifested itself as an anaphylaxis response to a bee sting. Meanwhile, it was me who was doing all the stinging.

Was it me who I was truly afraid of? Me who I was allergic to?

What else in our lives can trigger a severe and potentially life-threatening whole-body reaction?

- A feeling of lightheadedness
- Difficulty breathing
- Increased heartbeat
- Clammy skin
- Confusion and anxiety
- A loss of consciousness
- Disassociation from mind or body

These are the ego's favorite tricks. He pulls them out whenever we start to tread on his territory or when there might be a chance that he and his antics might get exposed.

Uh oh. Not that!

I'm not diminishing the *very* real and serious reactions listed above. They are scary, they hurt, and yes, they can and do occur. Yet, we have control over these reactions.

They are, ultimately, self-fabricated, self-induced protection mechanisms used by the ego to keep us and him safe. Out of the best intentions, of course.

The problem is that the ego cannot, and will never, see beyond himself. In all his best efforts to keep us alive and safe, he ends up hurting us. In ways that he will never understand or comprehend. Any effort here is futile as it's like hoping you can teach a two-year-old how to drive. It's just not going to happen.

Our job, our calling, is to open our eyes, our ears, and our soul to finding awareness. To recognize when the ego is, well, just being the ego. For all intents and purposes, he's just doing his job. This is why we must balance our reactions to these antics once we have an awareness of them. As we are now acutely attuned to what is happening and why, we can step into our power of choice. The choice to show the ego gratitude and appreciation for being on alert and doing all he can to keep us safe. And, at the same time, exercising our agency to choose a different reaction, a different feeling, or an alternative viewpoint. Once we are elucidated to these options, it becomes so much easier to be thankful that the ego exists and is in our lives.

"Our beliefs about ourselves and the nature of life are like a set of lenses through which we view the world," Marianne Williamson proffers in her magnificently epic book, *A Return to Love*. She goes on to explain, *"They shape our perceptions and our actions. If we believe we are unworthy, we will see evidence of our unworthiness*

everywhere. If we believe we are deserving of love, we will see evidence of love everywhere. If we believe we are helpless, we will see evidence of our helplessness everywhere. If we believe we are powerful beyond measure, we will see evidence of our power everywhere."

When we look at how to balance the ego with the Self, it becomes obvious that one does not preclude the other. The ego is not something for us to hate and shun; to ignore and constantly push away. It's about realizing that we are not *only* our ego. Yes, it is a part of us, but we have many layers. The ego is part of our worldly body, here to help us navigate this journey on Earth. It will not be coming with us after our time here. No matter what we believe happens after death, the egoic self will not be joining us.

It's worth revisiting the question of, *"What are you allergic to?"*

Where in your life are there areas of fear, of an allergic reaction, that dominate and strip control away from you? Where is it that you're left feeling incapacitated and incapable of moving?

I challenge you to sit and breathe into those questions. For whatever shows up, it may be helpful to write them down, journal about them or simply ruminate on them. The intent is not to solve what shows up for you but to sit in awareness with those thoughts and feelings. This is the first step and it's the hardest. Be honest and gentle with yourself as we move into a part of our journey together that requires a deeper level of vulnerability.

We are now touching our shadow side. And yes, the ego HATES this work. If any type of whole-body reaction shows up for you during the rest of our journey together (for me it's usually an intense tightening of the chest or stomach pangs) please pause, close your eyes, and take a few breaths.

You are safe.
Nothing can harm you in this moment.
You are simply reading a book.
The ego knows you are on a path to understanding and exposing it.
This is the threshold of the doorway, and you are about to step through it.
The ego is losing its grip, and he despises not being in control.
You are here to take back your power.
To take back your agency.
To own your choice.

"As humans, we tend to tell ourselves stories,
About how our life and circumstances are somehow harder/different than everybody else's.
A lot of people will even let these stories dictate their lack of action,
And ultimately cripple their potential in life.
The truth is your life is pretty amazing.
Yes, we all have our struggles.

Yes, things don't go the way we want sometimes.
Yes, it never gets "easy."
No, life isn't "fair" all the time.
...but the truth is...
You will likely have a few good meals today.
You likely have shelter, water, and most of all
OPPORTUNITY to improve your situation.
It's not as bad as you make it.
You know it. I know it.
The reality is you can change whenever you want."

- Andy Frisella

--- -- - *Deserving Better* - -- ---

Every time I think back to that serendipitous day in Los Angeles when I got seated next to Christine Hassler on that flight to Maui, I find myself shaking my head and smiling. It's not often that such a fortuitous moment finds us in life. At least not when we aren't paying attention or living with presence, as I wasn't at the time. What makes me smile most today though, is the uniqueness of who she is and how different the two of us are, and yet we found a way to connect instantaneously. She also opened my eyes to what I believe is one of the deepest papercuts that many of us give ourselves daily. Hence the focus of her work and her book, *Expectations Hangover*.

Expectations are so detrimental that they show up in the seminal work of Don Miguel Ruiz. In his book, *The Four Agreements,* they take a slightly different form, that of "assumptions." According to Ruiz, out of all the things that are beneficial or harmful to us, making assumptions makes the top four list. Assumptions can be particularly damaging in relationships, where miscommunication and misunderstandings can lead to hurt feelings, mistrust, and conflict. These relationships spill over into our work, social settings, and, strangely enough, every interaction we end up having with other humans.

Have you ever found yourself in a restaurant, trying to get the waiter's attention? With each passing moment of unsuccessful head nodding, eyebrow raising, and hand signaling, the tension inside of you builds and starts to boil your blood. They finally come over, all cheery-eyed and smiling, and you end up either blowing up at them or saying nothing while you order with intense irritation in your tone, head buried in the menu and unable to look them in the eye.

For me, I have deep rooted expectations about how people treat meetings. I recently had a doctor keep me waiting 27 minutes past our set appointment. I was irate. Not only had I missed, or was about to miss, another meeting, but I was on the verge of being late to pick up my daughter from school. When the doctor finally joined our virtual room, there was no apology or anything said but, *"So, what's been going on? What's not feeling good?"* Who did this doctor think she was? My expectations were shattered, and it led to me expressing myself in anger and frustration that I carried with me the rest of the day.

Granted, I didn't ask what her day was like. Or stop to find out that she was rushing back from having to run to the hospital for a last-minute emergency with an 8-year-old dealing with complications from leukemia. Or that, had she canceled our appointment, I wouldn't have been able to see another doc until the next day. Knowing this, she opted to be 27 minutes late and was trying to play catch-up, all in an effort to honor her patients, and do the best she could in the moment.

Let's not forget the very real impact this had on my day too. I got myself worked into such a tizzy that this frustrated energy carried with me throughout my day until just before dinner. All because of choice, my choice, to make an assumption and have expectations. Nothing of value came out of it for me, in fact, I arguably hurt myself, my colleagues, my kids, and anyone else I interacted with the rest of that day.

Entitlement works in much of the same fashion. This is because the three of these are interconnected linearly. Assumptions are the foundation for our expectations which drive us to feel entitled. Entitlement can't exist without an expectation, which means the two start to stack and it gets ugly, quickly. We're in a deep downward spiral before we know it. The power of choice lies within our empowerment. When we jump on the triple train of assumption-expectation-entitlement, we strip ourselves of our agency and are the cause of our own disempowerment.

German, being that he's from Uruguay, that's pronounced *"air"* and *"mon"* (the second part you have to say with a Jamaican accent), is one of those friends I've been with through thick and thin with. We are so different, yet that's what I adore about him. He's a creative genius and always brings a perspective to the table that is often counterintuitive to my own. I love him for this, even though it makes me want to punch him sometimes. I'm joking, but the friction between us, at times, is what allows the magic to appear. He and I both know it and we encourage our conversations to take us to that edge. The following was his story:

"Brent, my dad divorced my mom when I was nine. He left the country and struggled to find a solid place to live. He moved through South America, landing in the US for a few years and then, finally, to Israel. That's where he is today.

My sisters and I were left with my mom, which was also a toxic situation. She was dissatisfied with her life, and she took her frustration out on us kids, especially me. There was way too much verbal and physical abuse in our home. And it didn't stop there. Her choices on how she met life and showed up to it meant that she was rarely present, even when she was there physically. It was not good.

The last two to three years I feel like I have matured or am going through a midlife thing, and I am seeing things differently. I realized that I've been feeding myself a load of bullshit over the years, carrying a torch about how my early life was not so bad. Normal even. And in processing these feelings, it has allowed me to show myself some grace. To acknowledge how messed up it really was. At the same time, I am now aware that there were things in my mom's life that were really hard. I hadn't thought about them in that way before and I definitely don't agree with the way she chose to deal with them. I mean, coming home and hitting your child is never the answer. It's taken me almost 40 years to find compassion for her, as I now know that she never did, and still doesn't, have the tools needed to express herself in a healthy way.

As my dad moved around, he never helped my mom out financially, which only applied more pressure to the already strained relationship between my mom and us kids. My mom got remarried and, as you may have guessed, her "picker" is not the best. It turned out that this new guy had problems prior to marrying her and those issues bubbled up quickly. He had financial challenges stemming from unpaid loans and fraudulent checks. He was unable to get a bank account, so he started writing checks through my mom's account.

She trusted him and it destroyed everything. He left my mom without love to receive or to give. Yet in the end, it doesn't matter because there is no right answer. Simply the human being that she chose to be, just not according to her.

Enter entitlement.

Entitlement plays a significant role in our minds. Yes, you deserve better. Yes, you are entitled to expect more from that person, in that specific situation. But what do we do with entitlement? It's the first filter we turn to, and it can change the color of life for us.

In my mind, when somebody says, 'This person did something to me, and because of that, I'm allowed to or expected to react this way,' a built-in excuse is sitting there and waiting for us to grab it; we were wronged after all. If we were to walk away, then everyone would just think we let other people screw us over. Then lots of people would take advantage of us, and it would become a never-ending cycle of letting somebody else get the upper hand over us. This thinking leads us to believe we have only two choices. Bitch, moan, and complain like a victim or retaliate in the name of justice and protect our namesake (pride).

A third choice exists, whether we see it in the moment or not. When we make a conscious choice of giving someone the upper hand in a given situation, who really has the upper hand?

For me, entitlement is the belief that one has the right to act on an expectation. Entitlement is born from our expectations. I always think of the "code" that existed in the 1800s in the Old West. Should you find yourself in a saloon in 1827 and someone were to touch your wife's back, you were not only allowed and justified but expected to hit them with an empty glove across the face. Otherwise, you would be considered weak.

The society where you were born and raised, your parents, friends, school, and many other factors all influence the internal list of expectations that we carry with us. It becomes the code, the operating software of how we understand to interact with the world, forming the basis of our entitlements. Let's pretend that I'm a wife, and I feel like I should constantly be given roses. Every two weeks I have this expectation. You haven't delivered on what I feel entitled to, so now I guilt and shame you for it and am responding and treating you in a shitty way. All because my dad used to bring flowers to my mom every two weeks. I never knew that my dad was cheating on my mom. His guilt was heavy, which was why he was always bringing her flowers.

Having awareness of and understanding your code becomes super important. To understand what expectations are coming from outside, what entitlements are coming from within and being able to make choices through it all. I told my sister, 'You're entitled to hate our dad. He wasn't a dad to you. He didn't support our mom and he fled the country. But now you have a choice. Do you want to have a relationship with him for whatever time is left? You can still have a dad if you want to. If not, that's okay too. At least make your choice from a position of empowerment, instead of entitlement.'"

The lesson here was like a punch to my gut. I doubled over, trying to regain my breath. To know that we can make a decision that is not based on what an abandoned child should be entitled to or is expected to do is hard. Yet it's still a choice.

"It takes more energy to be someone you're not. It takes more strategy, more thought, more game plan. Behind any intent, there is expectation. You're hoping, wishing and seeking. And if you don't get the validation and approval you hoped for, you will internalize. You will judge yourself, causing your anxiety to skyrocket."

- The Angry Therapist

--- -- - *Similar Yet Different* - -- ---

"Hey Dad? Dad. Dad. DAD!
Did you see what I sent you on TikTok?" my teenage daughter shouted down at me from upstairs.

"No, dear. Remember, I turned off notifications for social media this year. So, nope, haven't seen it yet," I responded dryly.

"Dad. Dad. Dad! You really gotta check it out."

"Yeah, okay. Let me finish making coffee first."

She came bounding down the stairs, leaping every third step, nearly face-planting as she barely connected with the bottom step.

"You need to see this. Now!"

She pulled up her account and shoved her phone in my face. It was one of her friends, posing with her boyfriend, arm in arm, after a soccer match. Seemed harmless enough until I read one of the comments:

"I wonder if he knows what a dirty slut he's dating. She's just a druggie who has been cheating on him with lots of other guys."

I was aghast. I know the girl in the picture personally, her parents too, and she has been a good friend of my daughter for the past couple of years. Looking up I could see the confusion, compassion, rage, and fear welling up in my daughter's eyes. Somewhere in the back of her head, she knew that this could have just as easily been her and her boyfriend.

"*You wouldn't believe how often this happens, Dad,*" she blurted out. "*Just last week another one of my old jealous friends reposted a video I made and started blasting me on it. Making fun of my clothes, my hair, my forehead.*"

"*Yeah, we have to be so careful what we post because there are so many nasty comments that pop up. It's a big reason our generation has so much anxiety and depression,*" said Ty, my daughter's friend who had come over to hang out for the afternoon.

Not knowing exactly what to say or how to respond, I put my arm around them and gave them a big hug.

When did society at large become the judge, jury, and executioner? Telling us how to live, condemning us into oblivion with swift efficiency? It's impossible to even blink on social media without a bunch of trolling do-nothings chiming in with their negative overtones and assumptive all-knowing judgments. All while hiding behind a wall of technology, negating the need for actual eye contact.

These obvious aggressions are seriously damaging, and they are rampant. Not just on social media, but the news outlets as well. For that matter, it's everywhere. Movies, sitcoms, advertisements, podcasts, the list goes on forever. We are connected to each other, to the world, not only in breadth but at depth. I'm able to have a video conversation with my friend in Japan instantaneously and for free, all while discussing things that have typically been taboo. From health, wealth, relationships, emotional intelligence, parenting, childhood trauma, drugs, sex, etc. There is hardly a topic that is off-limits anymore.

There is great power at this level of access. We often take it for granted because it's literally at our fingertips whenever we desire to indulge ourselves. With great power comes great responsibility. Yeah, I know, not a new saying. Then perhaps we should act as if we not only knew about this saying but understood the gravity of it.

The responsibility I'm speaking of refers to remembering that not everybody wants the same thing in life. We don't value things in the same way and don't desire a life in the same fashion. I don't desire a penthouse in New York with a Rolls Royce because I desire to be connected with nature. For me, a seaside home in Guatemala with the ocean in my backyard and a rainforest in my front yard would be heavenly. Neither is better nor correct, it's just what I desire and appreciate versus what someone else does.

There is no wrong or right way to live life. Just what feels good for us and taps into our passion. The right path has little to no friction on it. It's natural, easy, comfortable, and makes us smile. And, odds are, this way is the absolute wrong way for someone else. So what?

When we judge or allow the judgments of others to influence us, we have already violated a sacred boundary with ourselves. Judging is nothing more than projecting one's own misery or failures onto someone else. It's ugly, it hurts, and it isn't real.

What is real is the stress and worry we allow into our world. This is where our choice comes in, or lack of it. We forget to be present and let the ego start projecting onto others or setting our boundaries too loose. We allow the projections of others to seep into the cracks of our boundary wall, oozing into our field of thought and making it that much more difficult to collect ourselves and get things back in order.

I often find myself worrying about other people before I worry about myself. Even though I am well aware that this is impractical and detrimental to my health, it's where my mind naturally goes. I can only assume it's similar for most of us.

With all this distraction and worry, it becomes virtually impossible to dodge the microaggressions that live just below the surface. Microaggressions work similarly to how thousands of negative choices over time affect us. They act as papercuts. Barely noticeable at the time of infliction but incredibly painful as they pile up.

What exactly are we talking about with regard to microaggressions? As adapted from *Sue et al., 2007*, they are the everyday slights, insults, putdowns, invalidations, and offensive behaviors people encounter during daily interactions with generally well-intentioned individuals who may be unaware that they have engaged in demeaning ways.

I find that this shows up most often when people start to meddle. The minute we interject ourselves into the decision train for someone else, especially without an invitation, we are treading on dangerous ground. Gaslighting becomes the inadvertent outcome, and all of a sudden, we are fully acting out of integrity in the most heinous of ways.

One of the best examples of this is something I learned in a master class group I was part of for seven years while holding the role of CEO at two different companies. When someone would bring an issue or topic to the group they were struggling with, it was against the rules to give them advice. We were only allowed to share a personal experience that had some relevance. The goal here was to allow the person with the issue to process it on their own and to come up with their own solution. By sharing an experience, we weren't telling them what to do or how to do it. It was a chance to try and relate to another human, empathetically and with compassion while maintaining our own perspective. The added bonus was that since the experience shared wasn't about the person with the issue, it was impossible to pass along a judgment or invalidate their feelings in any way.

Seth Godin addressed this in an extremely elegant way one day on his blog:

"There are countless ways to make a point. You can clearly demonstrate that you are angry, smart, concerned, stronger, faster or more prepared than the person you're engaging with.

But making a point isn't the same thing as making a difference.

To make a difference, we need the practical empathy to realize that the other person doesn't know what you know, doesn't believe what you believe and might not want what you want. We have to move from where we are and momentarily understand where they are.

When we make a point, we reject all of this. When we make a point, we establish our power in one way or another, but we probably don't change very much. Change comes about when the story the other person tells themselves begins to change. If all you do is make a point, you've handed them a story about yourself.

When you make a change, you've helped them embrace a new story about themselves. And even though it's more fun (and feels safe, in some way) to make a point, if we really care, we'll do the hard work to make a difference instead."

More often than not, when we make a point, we are engaging in microaggression. As Seth points out, making a point is just us flexing our muscles, showing our strength and exuding righteousness. Quite simply, it's us saying, *"I'm right and you're wrong."*

Being concerned with the way others choose to live their lives is nothing but a distraction. If we take a moment, look in the mirror, and bring the focus back to our lives, the misstep becomes apparent. The leaks in our own dam start to drip on us as well. Every time we concern ourselves with something or someone outside ourselves, we relieve the guards from their duty of patrolling from the parapets. Intruders are allowed in, and we end up receiving the same unnecessary medicine we are doling out.

Why do we fall into this trap so easily? Whether that's keeping verbal intruders out of our lives or to stopping intruding on others?

I suspect it has something to do with our survival instinct, fear of the unknown, the false need for power, and cultural conditioning.

--- -- - *Fallacy-ism* - -- ---

Growing up in Arizona, there were many opportunities to be around and ride horses. From the first time I put my foot in the stirrup and swung my other leg around and over the saddle, I felt comfortable. It was as though a natural connection existed, though I have no idea why. At most, I had a total of around ten hours in the saddle by the time I graduated high school. It wasn't until a few years later that I spent any significant time around them. And by significant, I mean one week a year.

My dad invited my brother and me to join him at a week-long men's retreat when we turned 21. Retreat is a generous word. It was more like a good 'ol boys club full of alcoholics, gambling, storytelling, and old west misogyny. I'd like to plead the fifth or play the "I was only 21 and didn't know any better" card here, but that would be a lie. I knew. I justified it as a week spent riding horses and bonding with my dad and brother. Mission accomplished in the latter part.

My brother (love you, Troy!) didn't seem to have the same ease with horses that came so naturally for me. He was always tense, on edge, and visibly uncomfortable as we mounted or dismounted. Every time the group quickened their pace to a fast trot, the look on his face was foreboding.

Each morning there were about eight different rides we could choose from. This particular day we chose a medium-length and difficult option. As we rode away from camp, the trail led us into a sandy creek bed and then had us working our way up a fairly steep embankment. There were about thirty of us in our trail group that morning, and we slowed to a crawl as, one by one, horse and rider leaped up the trail to climb to the ridge that was about 50 vertical feet above where we started. My dad was in front with my brother behind him and I brought up the rear.

After our dad made it to the top, he turned around and could see that my brother was a little nervous. Not to have his pride get the best of him, he dug his heels into the hindquarters of his horse. About halfway up the horse slowed, and you could see my brother fighting for control. He moved the reins back and forth and kicked harder now, but the horse wasn't having it. With one last rallying effort, my brother leaned forward just as the horse reared and tossed him off.

No one got hurt, luckily. Broken pride, some cuts, and a bad bruise were the worst of it. Or so I thought. The truth is my brother could've easily been killed that day. He was incredibly lucky and angry. He couldn't understand what he did wrong. He felt like he was confident and in control, but the horse just wouldn't listen to him.

Control is such a dangerous word.

How often have we either said or heard, *"Don't worry, I have everything under control."*

When was the last time you had control of something? Your car, you say? Oh, and then what happens when your brakes fail or a tire blows while going 75 mph? Okay, what about control over your money? How about what your significant other is feeling right now? Your order at Starbucks? None of those things? Shocking!

Control appears to be generally elusive. It begs the question: is control real at all? I mean, it has to be, right? How else can your boss make you show up at work and do a good job? Oh, right, he can't. Double eagle salute to him, you say? Nice. Way to take back control and show him who's the real boss.

A battle has been raging throughout time immemorial across every nation for control. From dynasties to nation states to religions to multinational corporations to natural resources to our bedrooms to _____ (insert just about anything). Humanity has normalized waging wars for control of whatever it is we deem important at the time. Wars! We kill for control and sleep well at night knowing it was justified.

Control, and who has it, consumes us as a civilization and has for millennia. From the highest levels of government down to what happens behind closed doors in our homes at night. It's a constant battle that starts with a bit of sarcastic wit, humor even, and usually ends in yelling, tears, or blood.

This is especially evident between teenagers and their parents. As a parent of teenage girls, one of the greatest struggles I've had is finding a balance between being their protector and coach and yet also letting them be their own person. In other words, learning to be a guide and not a dictator. Letting them "off the leash" and using gentle nudges instead of barking commands. It's not easy. Let me say that again, it's NOT easy. And, for the record, I have made about 8,379 mistakes along the way.

My daughter was Snapping (that's Snapchat for the plebes who aren't in the know, which included me six months ago) with one of her friends the other day. They were both 15 at the time, and I got a glimpse of their conversation. The friend had also shared a screenshot of a conversation she was having with her mom. It went something like this:

Paisy: *Let's go to lunch during your break. You have 2 hours before you have to be back at work, right?*

Friend: *Cool. You said your dad can take us?*

Paisy: *Yep. We'll pick you up at 2 pm and get you back by 3:30. How about Shake Shack?*

Friend: *My mom says no. Geez, what's her problem? Check out what she is saying...*

Friend's Mom: *I will pick you up at 2 pm*

Friend: *It's only going to work if Paisy's dad drives us.*

Friend's Mom: *That's not an option. I will be picking you up from your job. I can then pick up Paisy and take the two of you to lunch. Then I'll get you back to work before 4pm.*

Friend: *But Mom, Paisy's dad is already driving, and we have it all figured out.*

Friend's Mom: *It's not his responsibility to get you back to your job. I'm driving or you can't go to lunch. End of story!*

Friend: *Fine, then. I guess we won't go to lunch.*

Sounds silly and made up? Nope. This was a real conversation and it resulted in hurt feelings. If you look back on your own parenting or on your childhood, I bet there were more than a few instances of a similar dialogue and power struggle at play. This dance of one side wanting control, usually for reasons of allaying some sort of fear, and the other side desiring freedom along with the lack of being controlled.

Maneuvering through life's entanglements like this means that no one wins. The mom doesn't provide better protection for her daughter, nor does she teach her daughter some grand lesson about life. All she did was forfeit the choice she initially had, which was to share a life truth with her daughter, from a perspective of love instead of dictation. And her daughter ended up giving up the choice to have a nice afternoon and lunch with one of her best friends. Both of them lost the opportunity to listen to and be curious about the what and the why each of them was feeling at that moment. This resulted only in frustration and the addition of another layer of bricks on top of the wall that was being built between them.

Where is this desire or need for control, outside of what you can control (which is only yourself), at large in your life? Is it with your kids, your life partner, your boss, your teammates, your coach, the mailman, or your hairdresser?

As we attempt to apply force on the lever of control, we inadvertently lose control over our ability to choose. Isn't that an interesting conundrum? Our only real freedom in life, choice, is relinquished as we attempt to force control over someone else and ultimately take away their choice.

Attempting to hold onto control is like grabbing a hot cast iron pan off the stove and refusing to let go. Damn, that has to hurt!

Control is not a choice, it's a delusion, of the worst kind.

--- -- - *Land Mines* - -- ---

I feel compelled to disclose one of my most honed skills in life. I call it the "avoid then numb" tactic. I am a master at avoiding and then numbing so I don't have to feel anything or think about it. I've found it to be quite beautiful and effective for a long time. It's easy and quick, and I've mastered multiple methods that guarantee the same results every single time. I'm currently batting above a .900.

My mom used to say, *"You can't avoid things forever."* I have to call BS on that. There are lots of things that I have avoided my whole life, quite successfully I might add. The question here is not about avoidance, but at what cost. In the short term, the cost was a bottle of wine, some Italian cheese, and a little dark chocolate. It worked like a charm for many years.

Numb rhymes with dumb for a reason. The consequences here are serious and the subsequent hurt is deeper than we are prone to admit to. Pain at this depth is a good indication that our loved ones and friends are feeling it too, even when we pretend like we're hiding it and there's no way they could know. There is. If not directly, we are definitely peeing in the pool of their soul. It might take a while to build up, but it's salty and acidic, nonetheless.

Avoiding our feelings automatically hides our intelligence—intellectually, emotionally, and spiritually. Everything gets polluted.

The other hard truth is that we can't show up when we cover up. It's impossible to be fully authentic externally when we aren't fully authentic internally.

Avoidance is just one way we choose to ignore and pretend that something doesn't exist or isn't really happening. We all have a master's degree in the art of self-sabotage. It's part of growing up in today's world. And you thought that education wasn't free for the masses? Ha!

How many ways do we sabotage ourselves, you ask?

Negative self-talk	Focused on pleasing others
Procrastination	Not being able to say no
Perfectionism	Not taking responsibility
Fear of failure	Overthinking
Lack of self-discipline	Unable to hear criticism
Minimal self-awareness	Lack of self-trust
Resistant to change	Completely risk averse
Holding on to grudges	Not being assertive
Inability to set boundaries	Unable to embrace change
Being too hard on oneself	Not being able to forgive
Comparing oneself to others	Unhealthy balance in life
Lack of self-care	Closed-minded
Not learning from mistakes	Low communication skills
Failing to ask for help	Lack of setting priorities
Being too passive	Unable to let go of the past
Having expectations	Inability to manage emotions

We are so masterful at some of these techniques that it can be quite scary if we allow ourselves to take an honest look at things. Then we go (at least I do) and make it worse by flipping half of this list into ways that make us the victim.

Poor us. We have been wronged. Put down. Hurt. Damaged. Shit on.

Yes! Yes, we have.

No excuses. No "buts." Life is hard and it sucks at times. You can absolutely play the "I deserve better" card. It's your choice, as it always is.

Ding. Ding. Ding!
You've just won what's behind door #3.
A one-way trip down the direct path to suffering.
Go you. Yay!

Suffering is all around us. It feels unavoidable, inescapable, and ominous. And yet we sometimes need to allow suffering in so that we will be ready to confront our obstacles.

Our external world is always a reflection of our inner world. Everything we need to face, the obstacles blocking our growth, are already in front of us. We know it's there; we just aren't associating with it properly. More than likely the obstacle is right in front of our faces, staring at us, laughing, poking at us in jest. The first time we recognize one of these obstacles for what they really are, it can be a little unnerving. The simplicity and audacity of what they are can leave one in a state of bewilderment.

A few years back, my mother-in-law was driving me nuts. She was being a worrywart on an issue I wouldn't have thought twice about, or so I thought. There were phone calls, texts, emails, and social media shares. She was projecting her fears onto me and trying to get me to understand her position. It felt more like a rallying cry to switch sides and share the truth in what she believed. Honestly, it was obnoxious. At least, that's what I told myself.

The next morning, I sat with this frustration as I just couldn't shake it. I offered it up as something I wanted—no, needed—to release myself from. During my morning meditation, I asked the universe for help in how to show up calm, compassionate and to assist her in stopping the barrage. Over the next few minutes, as I went deeper into mental solitude, the insight I got left me flabbergasted. The way she was acting mirrored the way I was acting toward my business partner regarding a perceived challenge we were recently having with an employee.

Holy crap! This was my obstacle. A reflection of me and how I was showing up in my life and yet I couldn't see it. It was right under my nose. An issue I was dealing with daily and had allowed to become all-consuming. How did I miss this? How did I not see the connection point?

There was nothing to do other than accept ownership. That's the funny thing about awareness. Once you know, you know, and we can't un-know things, unfortunately. I apologized to my mother-in-law and my business partner, put a stop to my less-than-ideal handling of the situation at work, and addressed my personal challenges with the underlying fear that was at the root of both my behavior at work and my disdain for my mother-in-law's behavior.

The obstacle, it turned out, was the way (thank you, Ryan Holiday), and now it is no longer in my path. The next time we discover an obstacle in our inner world, all we must do is look externally, and it will make itself evident.

It's there, I promise. Just keep looking.

--- -- - *Groundhogs* - -- ---

I find it fascinating how our individual perspectives, attitudes, and experiences are constantly evolving. Regardless of any external factors, our own personal growth and development, as well as our responses to different situations are the only things that ever truly exert any influence over us. The "stuff" in our lives does not, in and of itself, bring about personal transformation; rather, it is the internal processes and reactions that we have to the things that can bring about such change. Molly Vass said it well in that, *"The stuff of our lives doesn't change. It is we who change in relation to it."*

During the process of writing this book, I finally made the switch over to everything Apple. I fought it for years, extolling the virtues of Windows and Android. There was no way I would ever give full control over to Apple and succumb to their closed-loop environment. No way was I going to give up the granular level of control that I thought only a PC could offer. Yeah, well, that's out the window. I now have a MacBook Pro, an iPad, and an iPhone.

Where is the face firmly planted in the hand emoji when you need it?

Part of what I feared was the transfer process. All my files, apps, systems and resources had to get updated, transferred and possibly transitioned into a new iWhatever version of it. As I was going through my emails and cleaning out the folders, I ran across one from my ex-wife. It was dated about one month before we got separated.

The first sentence was pure hatred, which was leaping off the screen. I stopped immediately as one of my boundaries was/still is not to allow that energy into my life. What's crazy is that I got an extraordinarily similar email two years later, almost to the day, which was also over a year since we had been officially divorced. I was shocked that two years later, nothing had changed. I had to stop and give myself some kudos. There was pride in being able to stop and honor my boundary, which doesn't always happen.

My hands off the keyboard and eyes closed, trying to get recalibrated, I looked back down and saw that the preceding email was something I had written. Having caught my eye, I skipped over the part that she wrote and started skimming my portion. It was my tone and my style, but I couldn't recall the content for the life of me. This was weird. What the heck was I blabbering on about?

That's when it hit me. This email wasn't from 2021, it was from 2011. Ten years and nothing had changed. Not the tone. Not the message. Not the lack of love or respect in our relationship.

After rereading what I had written, the setup to that angry response, I realized that I was stronger than I thought, even way back then, but I clearly didn't trust myself. Instead, I numbed, I avoided, and I/we let it go on for another decade. To be clear, this is not a one-sided issue. I played my role and am not using this platform as a chance to pass the blame. The bottom line is that parts of our relationship were toxic, and it went on for way too long. Without ever realizing it before, I felt like Bill Murray in the movie *Groundhog Day*. Same shit, different day. Only my memory seemed to get wiped, probably from my excessive numbing with alcohol, during my nightly dream state. Apparently, my morning yawn and stretch were like shaking the etch-a-sketch of my marriage.

"Oh, another blank slate. Cool. Let's codependently create something!" I can just hear my hurt little boy of an inner child chirping at me from my right shoulder.

More delusions. Not of the healthy kind.

What's tough is that even these unhealthy delusions are born from a place of protection. Our ego (little boy/girl, inner child) is operating out of our best interest, or what it believes is in our best interest. Our bodies are programmed to automatically respond to fear and cut us off from our truth, even when that truth is staring us in the face. Fear causes us to get stuck on the never-ending merry-go-round of creating and choosing unhealthy delusions in order to feel safe and protected.

These patterns are everywhere if we start to pay attention. Many of our mental health disorders are riddled with these circular behaviors that spin the inflicted person into a downward spiral. Of course, the same thing can and does happen to all of us. Especially when we aren't paying attention and in ways we don't even notice. It even creeps up on us through our family history, handed down, just like Aunt Gertrude's gap in her front teeth. Thanks, Gerty!

While this isn't the type of inheritance most of us are pining for, there's no escaping it or giving it back. Physical features are easy to recognize, yet there's so much we don't know about what else has been passed down to us. Intergenerational transmission, as it's formally known, is a portal for all kinds of lovely things to be shoved into whatever closet (or pillowcase) we keep our skeletons in without us being the wiser.

If this is news to you, and I certainly hope it's not, then it's time to get cozied up with and catch the ear of the elders in your extended family. In addition to physical, biological, and psychological ailments, this portal opens us up to traumas, addictions, inappropriate or unwelcome behaviors, ticks, nagging tendencies, and all sorts of other personality traits being passed on that none of us want or need. Having a long talk with Aunt Gertrude could be quite enlightening as it might reveal the genesis of unidentified shame, guilt, distrust, anger, money, low self-esteem, fear, etc.

One way it can show up is like it did during a chat I had with my friend Lindsay:

"I have these weird money blocks that I don't, for the life of me, know where they came from," groaned Lindsay. *"I grew up with more than enough. Not that we were millionaires, but we didn't want anything. We had what we needed, and then some, and we were well cared for."*

"Where does that show up in your life today?" I wondered.

"Even though I wasn't raised this way, I find myself hoarding money. This isn't new, though. All through my childhood I did the same thing. When I got money, no matter the reason—birthday, babysitting, allowance - I socked it away and wouldn't spend any of it."

"Is that really that abnormal? I mean, I did the same thing, at least until I was able to drive. Then it all went to hell. Literally!"

"Ha! Brent, I hear you. Let me give you an example. I was in the store with my mom one day, and there was a doll that I really wanted. It wasn't overly expensive, and my mom caught me staring at it. 'You've saved your money so well,

and you have plenty of it. Go ahead and buy the doll. It's worth it as I know you'll love playing with it.' But I couldn't do it. It used to drive her crazy.

Of course, there were times when I would buy the item, whatever it was, and then I immediately felt distraught. Like I was a horrible person, but I was just a kid. All of this over a flippin' Barbie doll. I would drive myself to the point of insanity."

"That sounds really intense, Lindsay, as if your whole person was immersed in the deep emotions and corresponding feelings that this evoked."

"It was overwhelming. A kid shouldn't have these types of feelings and emotions."

"Lindsay! There you go shouldering on yourself again. You are and were doing your best. Can you find some grace for yourself in there?"

"*I know, I know,*" Lindsay sighed. "*It was all so confusing. I kept asking myself, 'Why are you carrying this heavy burden that clearly isn't yours?' My mom and I started discussing where this might exist in our lineage, and it led me to my great-great-grandma. I don't have all the answers yet, but I am hearing bits and pieces of a forgotten story riddled with trauma. It reeks of betrayal, physical abuse, and abandonment. Though I may never know the exact story or the true origin, it has become clear that I am not the only one in my family that has had to deal with this passed-down trauma.*

I can't begin to tell you the breakthroughs I have had since finding this out. It's like the chains are broken and I can finally breathe. Like my choice is available to me once again. My power is finally back!"

I did a deep dive into myself, thanks to Lindsay's vulnerability with me. Turns out, both of my parents have their own generational based traumas. I'm still working through exactly what is showing up on my dad's side, but what was on my mom's side was ugly. She didn't know how to process it, and although it was unintentional, she carried it forward into her own life—and subsequently into mine. My mom kept her mouth shut for 20 years even though she knew my dad was cheating on her. She pretended like it wasn't happening and put her head in the sand. Just like me.

What I've learned is that there was a choice, or a lack of one, on my part, allowing the shit show to go on for over ten years in my marriage. Like my mom, I stuck my fingers in my ears and closed my eyes. The delusion I chose to accept as truth was that I was a martyr, doing it all in the last-ditch effort to see if we could make it work and possibly preserve the sanctity of our family, yet all it did was end up hurting myself, my wife (ex-wife now), and my kids. This was a lesson in surrender and how to let it all go. It was the past, after all, and letting it cycle back through my life or my kids', over and over again, wasn't helping anyone.

All of this triggered a much older wound for me that I was unaware I was still harboring. I went to a small Christian school during my elementary years, and it was filled with lots of trauma. It feels like there was endless judging, guilt, shame, and bullying.

The moment most deeply etched in my memory happened in my 7th grade year during spirit week. The whole school was out on the field participating in a decathlon of events. One kid, Steven, always seemed to have a chip on his shoulder and was definitely part of the cool kid crew. He had messed with me multiple times over the previous year and the tension was building between us. He seemed to grow in stature and power every time he found a way to embarrass me publicly.

This particular day, we were out on the soccer field participating in five different track and field events. As we stood there, Steven went behind my brother, who was two grades below me, and pulled down his pants all the way to his ankles. I immediately ran over and shoved him. He stumbled and caught himself, narrowly avoiding falling on his butt. He charged back at me, and a teacher stepped in to intervene. Though I am not sure why, all three of us got sent to the principal's office.

When we got there, the principal didn't do anything. She wanted to "pray" about it, hold hands, and perform some sort of kumbaya—everybody loves everyone and turns the other cheek like Jesus did—seance. My mom lost her shit and pulled us out of that school three weeks later. I never did forgive Steven; at least not for another 25 years. I also never dealt with how it felt to be bullied, which is probably why it happened again by a guy named Brian in 8th grade and then again by another (different) Steven in high school.

I find that the deeper I go, the more intertwined these memories are with many things that I have struggled with over the years. They are deeply woven into the fabric of my story and I well up with tears every time I go there.

--- -- - *Reflecting* - -- ---

I pulled on my trail shoes and jumped in the car. Getting into nature and going vertical is how I hit the reset button. When I got to the top of the mountain, I scanned the horizon, found the setting sun, and plopped down on the flat edge of a boulder. Closing my eyes, I let the wind whip across me and cool down the sweat dripping from the sides of my face.

Rooting my feet into the dirt and deliberately slowing my breath, I felt a surge, a deep power within. Knowing that it was my time and my right to stop pussy footing around. To manifest and design what it is I desire. To create more of it. To receive it as a gift. To embrace and relish it. To cherish it. To put an end to decades, if not centuries, of intergenerational hand-me-downs. No more!

I had a choice. I have a choice. It's up to me alone to put an end to the unhealthy patterns in my life.

PAPERCUTS

Chapter 7:
LEARNING TO FLY

"Guilt is the bite that injects the venom of shame."

- Me

--- -- - *Craftsmanship* - -- ---

Humans don't always make sense to me, including myself most of the time. We have such selective hearing, seeing, and believing. We live in an ever-morphing illusion, where the choice of how to interpret our interactions within the illusion becomes our delusion.

These choices almost always come down to love or fear. What we fail to recognize is that love and fear exist on the same spectrum. They're opposites yet the same all at once. The polarity here means we have the ultimate choice, and we can't make a wrong choice. However we choose, our reality becomes truth. Truth only for us, though. Remember, it's our chosen delusions that provide the evidence for truth.

Wait a minute. A fact is indisputable, no matter whose illusion it's part of. It's like a desk in a room. It just is!

Yes, and facts are virtually nonexistent and rarely play a role in our stories.

What? Why? This makes no sense.

A truth and a fact are the same thing, save one little, tiny thing. Both can be proved in some way, with objective research, calculations, or experience. Truth, and only truth, has the added element of belief.

This is what makes truth individualistic and subjective. Personal even.

I implore you to really let this sink in. How often do we use fact and truth interchangeably? Not only in your conversations but with our thoughts, internal stories, and beliefs.

This is why we have phrases such as, "What's your truth?"

It could be why we are masters at forcing our truth on others. We even demand that they see our truth as THE truth. Of course, there's no such thing. Truth involves feelings and beliefs that we often can't explain. We simply just know. And those feelings and beliefs are for us. Yes, only us. In solidarity. My truth is not your truth. There is no amount of convincing or arm twisting that can make anything else so.

Truth is governed by polarity. It has to be. How else can your truth and my truth be different yet exist simultaneously? How can I know, without a doubt, that milk is <u>not</u> good for the human body and yet you know the opposite to be true? It comes down to our experiences. Our interactions with reality. Our interpretation of what our senses relay back to us along with our beliefs. Milk makes me feel horrible, and I usually have to run to the toilet. It might provide you with needed calcium and make you feel like you have stronger bones. Both are true. Both are valid. Both are delusions.

Welcome to reality!

Here it is. Another papercut caused by choice. Or not. Does this frustrate you? Do you find you are annoyed? Or are you excited and feeling giddy with a subtle joy lingering on the back of your tongue?

I choose joy for a very specific reason. For me, it's validation that we are in control of something. That we have power. That nothing is predestined. Choice always exists at every juncture. It's like one of those children's books where you choose A or B and then go down the next rabbit hole until the story splits again. Both endings exist simultaneously. And we can get there from multiple angles and routes.

Life is a paradox. On all levels. In all ways. Always.

It's part of the DNA of our definition. The design of life as we know it. Personally, I wish it was less confusing, and yet I love that this design is perfect. It's beyond our ability, as humans, to truly hold a level of comfort around this topic.

Paradoxes are confusing by design. They are the hidden power of the universe.

If you don't fully get it, have some internal confusion, or just feel like there's still more to understand here, good! That means humans are reading this book and not just AI bots. You are normal. You are perfect. And, while you may be a child of or a fractal of God, you are not God.

I've had to make peace with the fact that I won't ever understand the most complex topic known to mankind. While we may get to a point where we can embrace the great paradox, it will never be something we are fully comfortable with. Not only are we not supposed to be, we also weren't designed to be. There's a natural tension that exists for good reason. "*Let it be*," were some apropos words of wisdom from Paul McCartney. Take solace in knowing that you can fully trust yourself and that your truth is your guide.

"The greatest fear in the world is of the opinions of others. And the moment you are unafraid of the crowd you are no longer a sheep, you become a lion. A great roar arises in your heart, the roar of freedom."

- Osho

And freedom creates a space where we can step into our choice. To step into the uniqueness that we each possess. This is what defines us and our truth.

We are all artists.
Painting on the canvas of illusion.
With colors and shapes of our choosing.
Creating our own unique delusion.
We are all artists.
The masters of our lives
Artists of self-delusion.

We are artists. Crafting our delusions. Based on our individual truths.

This is worthy of great celebration!

You may be one in seven billion, but no one has what you have, believes exactly as you do, or will ever occupy your brain, spirit, or body. You and you alone are the only one who gets this unique experience. Smile! Breathe deep and fill your lungs, holding it at the top. Close your eyes and be thankful. You are alive and present in this moment!

You are in control, if you choose to be.

Actually, we're always in control. We might just be in deferral mode. Allowing our reptilian brain to run amuck and live in constant fear. A heightened state of alert or emergency, flooding your system with chemicals designed to save our life, not run our day. Eventually leading to a shutdown, where the subconscious, ergo the ego, takes the reins and lets the reticular activating system (this is like our own built-in artificial intelligence) choose for us.

This, friends, is the path to where we get stuck in life. When we aren't creating, stepping into our inner artist, owning our power of choice and expressing it to the world, we open ourselves up and are vulnerable to getting hurt. Usually by hurting ourselves.

We start making hundreds of decisions daily that cause harm over time. Like little, tiny papercuts all over our bodies. Our choices influence our beliefs which shape our worldview and influence our behavior. If we consistently make decisions based on false beliefs, we may be acting in ways that are not aligned with our truth, which can lead to negative consequences. Notice that I said, *"our truth"* and not *"the truth."* Our pain and suffering stem from misalignment. This happens where and when we are not living in alignment with our own truth.

"Assumptions, judgments, and expectations are the tints that define the color of paint we are brushing on the house of our soul."

                                                     - Unknown

When we believe that we are not capable of achieving certain goals, we may not even attempt to pursue those goals, leading to missed opportunities and potential regrets.

Similarly, if we believe that we are not deserving of love or respect, we may engage in self-sabotaging behaviors or accept mistreatment from others, leading to feelings of low self-worth and unhappiness. Over time, the accumulation of these psychological papercuts is guaranteed to take a toll on our mental and emotional well-being, potentially leading to more serious mental health issues such as depression or anxiety.

According to the World Health Organization, almost one billion of us are living with a mental disorder, with anxiety and depression being the most common. In 2020, thanks to the COVID-19 pandemic, there was a 26% and a 28% rise in anxiety and depressive disorders respectively. These numbers don't take into account the billions of us that experience acute anxiety and depression on a sporadic basis. It's just as real and painful in the moment as it is for those that are clinically diagnosed. Anxiety and depression are insanely overwhelming, painful, and straight-up debilitating.

PLEASE! Stop giving away your power. This is what happens when we let fear rule us and we stop owning our choice. It's scary, it sucks, and it's very real. And the frustrating part is that we are only hurting ourselves. One of the guys in a mastermind group I'm part of, Mike Brcic of Wayfinders, once said, *"It's easy to fall into a dominant narrative of what it means to live a human life and easy to forget that ours is but one interpretation."*

Hopefully, by now, we have a clear understanding of who we are, where we've been, and what we desire going forward. I remind myself daily, *"Don't look back, you're not going that way."* Pushing forward from here requires us to show up, trust ourselves, and put one foot in front of the other.

Becoming a master at our craft, our art, is the journey we are currently on together. The road is bumpy, beyond difficult at times, and also incredibly rewarding.

This is not the road to happiness.

This is the happiness road.

--- -- - *Dull Blades* - -- ---

For my 10th birthday, my uncle got me a Bowie knife. At just over fifteen inches long, it's one of the bigger hunting knives out there. My uncle knew what every little boy wanted, and he nailed it. It even had my name etched on a plate that was glued onto the deer antler handle. There was something primal about it. Powerful. I can't really explain why—it just was.

My mom didn't quite exude the same level of excitement. Let's just say that I wasn't even allowed to look at it, let alone hold it. The longing I had to keep it in my room and on display was a laughable thought. The thing I didn't understand about my mom's serious freak out about this gift was that the knife wasn't sharp. The steel blade was completely dull. In my mind, there was no danger.

My uncle said that this was so I could choose what type of edge I wanted when I got old enough to use the knife. He had a booklet that described all the different honing options available. A booklet! I was beside myself. How could there be so many unique ways to put an edge on a knife? Lots of possibilities existed but none of them made the blade sharp today. I couldn't wrap my head around my mom's hesitation.

Let's just say that the knife vanished from my room and showed back up a few years later. It was randomly there, on my desk, when I got home from school one day. As I picked it up and rolled it around in my hands, I was mesmerized by the sensations that pulsed through my veins. There was a kinetic energy, a coiled power, that was stored in this piece of steel. It wasn't even a knife, for all intents and purposes, yet, but it would be soon enough. All I had to do was decide how I wanted to sharpen it.

The knife was so big and so cherished by me that it was overwhelming to think about what to do and how to do it. What if I chose wrong?

My uncle asked me, *"What don't you want?"*

I knew that I didn't want it to be 100% serrated as that wouldn't be very versatile. I also didn't want just another sharp knife, like my other hunting knives.

I had plans. Big plans for this bad boy of a man's knife. It had to cut a steak, because who doesn't need a 15" long knife to cut steak with? It also had to function as a hammer, tree saw, bone crusher, and a few other backwoods related do-it-all aspirations that I had.

After a couple of weeks, I finally figured it out. A standard sharp edge with serration on the bottom at a 70/30 ratio. Then a brass sheath on the back of the blade to allow for hacking and hitting. Everything I had dreamt about was about to become a reality.

Later that summer my dad, brother and I went camping. Looking back at pictures today, I looked ridiculous. At the time, though, I thought I was so cool, so manly, with this massive knife slung off the right edge of my belt. Let's just say that I got my money's worth. That knife got about 20 hours of use in just three days. On our way home, my dad asked me questions about my plans to sharpen the knife. I had seen him use a pumice stone on some of our cooking knives before, but he cautioned me that each type of blade, whether steel or another metal, needed a specific type of sharpener.

I decided to ignore his advice and shoved the knife under my bed. The following spring, we were getting packed up to go camping again, and at the last minute, I remembered to look under my bed, hoping this was the location where I had stashed my pride and joy. Yes! Knife in hand, we headed out for a long weekend in the woods.

Shocking but not surprising, when I pulled the knife out of the sheath, it had a crusted layer of rust on it. I asked my dad why, and he said some blades are made of steel and require a little bit of oil rubbed on them to keep them sealed from the air. Huh. Well, shoot. I cleaned it off the best I could and put it away. That night we had steaks and out came my way too big—but it didn't matter because it was so cool—knife. Only something was wrong. These steaks were impossible to cut through. *"Did you buy the cheap steaks, Dad?"* I blurted out.

"No, son," he said with a smile. *"Did you sharpen your blade after the last trip?"*

The words of wisdom that I had ignored those months ago came flooding back in. How could this be? The knife was basically brand new, only having been on one camping trip. I bowed my head and spent the evening pouting and sulking. This was so stupid. I couldn't believe that this was happening to me.

I have found myself in this same place, with the same feelings, many times in my life. Curious about what has me stuck. Why I am not as effective as I usually am. Sleeping more than normal. Motivation lacking. Finding myself unable to execute with speed or precision. Missing the joy and lightness that comes from socializing. Wondering where my passion had gone and what I was doing with my life.

Just like the weather, our lives are seasonal. We ebb and flow, wax and wane, often without our direct knowledge. I find myself oblivious to these slow movements most of the time. No different than, with the exception of sunrises and sunsets, how I forget that we are constantly rotating at roughly 1,000 miles per hour.

Similar to how a steel knife or cooking pan will slowly rust without constant care, our lives require this same commitment to attention. Arguably at the much higher level of a persistent cadence. A rhythm that we conscientiously build into our lives to address the four pillars of who we are:

SPIRITUAL: surrendering to something greater than ourselves
INTELLECTUAL: pursuing knowledge and a path to understanding
SOCIAL: connecting with others and building community
PHYSICAL: maintaining a healthy and active body

The best part is that there are no rules here, which allows us the distinct advantage to step into our choice and create. We iterate as we see fit in the moment. And when our edge becomes dull, we can replace it with an entirely new one. Going from a serrated to a straight edge or the other direction. We have the ultimate choice, and no one can stop us!

Now that we have this awareness, it is our responsibility to keep that edge sharp. Even if we desire to change it in the future, there is no reason not to keep it in tip-top shape until the exact second we want something different. Being cognizant of how sharp we are keeping ourselves across all four pillars takes effort, yet this effort is minimized when we incorporate a consistent cadence of upkeep. Scheduled maintenance, of sorts.

Each pillar has its own frequency, and each of us, individually, has our own needs within each of these. Some of us go to church every Sunday. My routine is to meditate twice a day for 15-20 minutes. Others of us hit the gym three days a week. I like to hike, ride my bike, do yoga, and get in some curls for the girls (sorry, dumb guy joke). There is no one prescription that is a catch-all for everyone.

Find your edge. Define it. Set "Yes You CAN" goals and then build out your schedule of maintenance. That might be hourly, daily, or weekly. Odds are it isn't less frequent than weekly. Here's where awareness comes in (and yes, awareness is the entire point of this conversation).

The sharper we are in each of these four pillars, the more awareness we have about who we are, what's going on around us, and how we are showing up. We sense the papercuts early on, shift our behaviors, and do it differently the next time. We are more attuned to our bodies and can feel the obstacles, like detecting cancerous spots in the early stages and cutting them out.

For maybe the first time, we are present, showing up for life and ourselves. Our energy is turned inward, and we find joy, fulfillment, and peace in nurturing our edges. Keeping them intentionally razor-sharp.

There is no greater gift we can offer the world, outside of mastering our thoughts, emotions, and actions. We endeavor to show up for our families, partners, jobs, friends, and the world in general as the best version of ourselves.

Of course, this looks different from day to day. Duh. We're only human (thank God). Sometimes it vacillates from minute to minute. All of which is okay. In fact, it's more than okay, it's perfect. When we are present, in each of life's moments, then we are doing our best in that moment.

"But I sure don't feel like I'm doing my best right now," says a mopey you.

Compared to what? When? At each moment you are always only doing your best.

"Wait a minute, you said I always have a choice, that I have agency over my life?"

Yes, I did. And you're right, you always have agency. If you choose it instead of giving it away.

"You have me thoroughly confused. How can I have agency, which means I can choose how to show up, and yet I'm showing up lackluster and it's somehow perfect?

You're saying it's the best I can do, even when I know it isn't?"

Exactly! Let me explain. Nobody ever shows up to life purposely, with effort, trying to do their absolute worst. To act in a way that showcases their flaws and how imperfect they are. We may feel overwhelmed, tired, depressed, or incapable of doing any better at the moment, lacking the energy needed to spring out of our current funk. It's all perfect.

Gently tell the inner critic to chill out.
You've got this.
Even when you don't.

--- -- - *Tinnitus* - -- ---

"In life, you're going to say and do things that anger some, but encourage others. What upsets one person will be exactly what uplifts another. This is why you can't take criticism too seriously. Because if all you do is listen to the negative, you'll miss out on all the positive. You'll end up apologizing for the wrong things, neglecting to say the right things, and ultimately, living a life that is far from the life you truly wish to be living."

- **Kyle Creek aka "The Captain"**

Ever since I can remember, there has been a dull, high-pitched ringing in both of my ears. For years I've explored whether it is sensory-induced, food-triggered, emotionally driven, or any other derivative of external or internal stimuli. Nothing reduces it, except for meditation. But that's only a temporary fix. Within two to three hours, it's back again.

I am acutely aware of when it gets exacerbated. Every time I get stuck in my left brain, the intellectual know-it-all side of myself that likes to reason its way through life; it happens. Boom (I mean ring?)! The internal volume ratchets up 20 decibels. Usually this means that my ego, the small self, has taken the reins and is about to go on a critical rant.

The inner Judge, that son-of-a-bitch of a critic, is so strong in some of us that the sound is deafening. For me it's a constant ringing. For you it might be a loud blabbermouth that just won't shut the heck up. My buddy in Austin yelled out, *"Shut up, Klaus,"* in the middle of our conversation one day. *"Oh, sorry,"* he said. *"Klaus is my inner critic. I named him after a German Shepard we used to own who would never stop barking."* The annoyance of this critic can be at epic levels. I get it! Finding a way to drown out the noise has never worked for me. Anything I've tried that seemed promising turned out to be a temporary fix at best.

My inner voice is chirping at me, *"Are you saying that we're just stuck? That this voice will always be there and there's nothing we can do?"*

Not exactly. It's true that it's always there. It's a part of who we are after all. But that doesn't mean it needs to rule our thoughts, our life, or our choices. It's there to protect us, even though it often delivers the opposite results. Acknowledgment and thankfulness go a long way with the Judge. Oddly, so does logic. It's one of the few parts of our inner world that respects and responds to a well-formed argument. To keep him at bay, I often turn to history, as there are countless world leaders that have said it better than I could.

"Comparison is the thief of joy" is a phrase commonly attributed to Theodore Roosevelt, the 26th President of the United States. Roosevelt also spoke about the dangers of comparing ourselves to others and the importance of focusing on our own progress and achievements. In a speech he delivered in 1910, he said,

"It is not the critic who counts; not the man who points out how the strong man stumbles, or where the doer of deeds could have done them better. The credit belongs to the man who is actually in the arena, whose face is marred by dust and sweat and blood; who strives valiantly; who errs, who comes short again and again, because there is no effort without error and shortcoming."

When we compare ourselves to others, we are automatically being held back by fear of failure. We let self-doubt creep in and get a foothold. We lose access to our voice, our story, and the ability to share experiences, thoughts, and feelings freely and purely. Shrinking so far into the shadows that our communication is relegated to absolute necessity only.

One of the most powerful tools we have as humans is our ability to verbally communicate with one another. It sets us apart from other animals and enriches our interaction with one another. We have been able to accomplish incredible things over the course of history thanks to this skill.

NOTE TO SELF:
I am responsible for what I say.
I am *not* responsible for what is heard.

It's easy to forget that verbal communication is also our most limiting quality. Often, we aren't able to "put into words" what we are feeling. We stumble on finding the perfect descriptive word for something we see, hear, taste, smell, or feel. Our senses pick up on nuances that we just can't do justice to with our command and use of language.

Dance, acting, and music are all forms of communication that can touch the deepest parts of our souls. They can access places that words could never come close to unlocking. Have you ever found yourself bawling at your local movie theater, enthralled and at the edge of your seat during a ballet, or energized and pumped out of your mind, thrashing your head and playing the air drums at a Metallica concert? Words simply fall short and flat of being able to describe these experiences, especially as it applies to the emotions they trigger in us and the resulting feelings that emanate throughout our extremities.

Descending two short flights of stairs, I entered a basement bar of a well-known seafood and steak restaurant. As I skirted past the hostess, a lobster tank enticed patrons to be in control over choosing their meal while highlighting how fresh it would be. The smell was all I could think about. How was I going to spend the next 90 minutes sitting twenty feet from this open-air tank and enjoying the appetizer and beverage I was about to order? I'm quite sure that lobsters coming straight out of the ocean don't smell like they do in this tank.

Plugging my nose while sipping a glass of Rioja, I settled into being present for my friend, who desperately needed to get some things off his chest. Our whole conversation started because we were discussing his passion and hobby as a musician in his spare time. He loves guitars. So much so that he built one for himself. Two, if my memory serves me right. He writes music and finds solace in the creative space that he is whisked off to every time he picks up a guitar. He disclosed to me that never once, not in 15 years of marriage, had his wife ever asked him to play his guitar for her.

"*I need it,*" he said as he stumbled to get the words out, anger flashing in his eyes. "*I need it because I can't stand the way she thinks she can go around loving people the way she wants. She needs to learn to love people the way they are. With the gifts they have and how they show up. And I want my wife to be a big enough person to go there instead of being lazy and just loving everybody in her way. It speaks to the effort she is willing to put into this relationship. Why am I with somebody if I am not loved and respected for who I am and what I need?*"

His pain was palpable. It hurt him to the very core of who he believes himself to be. He also has never shared his feelings about this topic with her. When I asked him why, he said, "*Because she should just know. I spend months cutting wood, sanding, painting, and stringing the guitar in our garage. My office has guitars hanging on the wall. I play almost every day. Even my friends know how important this is to me.*"

How often, I wonder, do we fail to communicate? Particularly in those moments where things seem beyond obvious? Our relationships are riddled with assumptions and expectations, mired in codependency.

This topic has been at the core of my journey. Truly understanding how a relationship, romantic or platonic, can function where neither side actually needs anything from the other side. Yet together, individual growth is supported, and experiences are enhanced. Something tells me this is a lifelong practice to truly understand and get good at this dance.

Personally, I have given away too much power in relationships and expected things in return, mainly happiness, that was never theirs to give. Truly being happy with who I am as is (no car, house, clothes, friends, body shape, etc.) has been so interesting to investigate and play with. I am finding that the more I trust myself, the more I love myself, and the more I find happiness (and gratitude) in who I am, the fewer expectations I have, the more curious I can become, and the more happiness is found when interacting with others.

Co-creation, in any relationship, becomes an experience enhancer, not a necessary function of happiness or joy. We can start to replace codependency with learning how to co-create, while leaning into the knowing deep in our gut that we don't need the other person. We simply appreciate how they show up in our life and the space they hold for us to trust ourselves. Our inherent fulfillment seeks out a need and steps in to lend out this gift for the purpose of synergy. In creating a whole that is more valuable than the parts, no different than a viola prodigy sitting down and playing with a fifty-five-person orchestra.

Stepping fully into what possibilities co-creation holds for us shines a spotlight on the unique power of choice we hold. Whether we see this as a gift or a burden, it's ours to acknowledge and accept. Ours to own. To ignore and suppress or embrace and rejoice. It could be said that the biggest sin (though I don't believe in such things) is to give away our power to choose. To hand that agency to someone or something else.

Is our fear that great? Is our trust in ourselves that low?

Has love been vanquished from its throne of being the one and only true force in our lives?

--- -- - *Inner Trust* - -- ---

"***Integrity*** is the cure for psychological suffering. Period."

- **Martha Beck**

It all begins with our eyes wide open. Our ears perked up. Our hearts breathing in and out the energy around us. Feeling into these spaces, the dark and dirty corners that we have always ignored. Here we will find all the places and moments where honesty has slipped past us, like a warm breeze that rustles our hair and then is gone. It was nothing, right? Almost as if it never happened. A fleeting moment leaving nothing behind in its wake, or so it seems.

We make light, slough off and dismiss these moments, just as easily as we throw a plastic water bottle in the trash. It was minuscule. It means nothing in the grand scheme of things. Maybe.

How many times did your mom give you that look of disapproval with the slightest hint of guilt and a smokey layer of shame loosely wisping around it? I deserved it. At least that's what I told myself. Meanwhile, 40 years later it still sits like a stack of bricks on my shoulders, gently influencing the way I respond to my daughters, my coworkers, and friends.

It's the big things that matter after all. The big bad black lies that we would be remiss to cover up or spin. But the little white lies aren't even lies, they're story fillers. We all do it and for good reason. We don't want to hurt others, so we withhold the tiny details. The unimportant ones. All the stuff that isn't particularly relevant and won't change the outcome anyways.

Those.

Yes, those forgotten and dismissed nothings are the thousands of papercuts that lead to our deepest wounds. It doesn't take years upon years either. Our ability to tell white lies, spin our stories, and leave out key details, which we pretend don't matter, is obnoxious. I know because I was a master at this. All the little things that actually matter most. We are bleeding from these cuts and they're all over our bodies. Yet we don't even notice them because the blood isn't gushing out from one spot alone. Band-Aids won't help or even work. The wounds are too small. Too spread out. Too shallow.

My friend asked me the other day, *"What is preventing you from living in integrity today?"*

My answer was, *"My ego. My lack of unconditional love for myself. Specifically, I have let it block intimacy in my romantic relationships and am regularly showing up in my head instead of in my heart."*

This same friend called me a month later during a break she had from the intense travel required for her speaking career. After some friendly hellos and a brief catching up, I asked, *"What simple truth (or fallacy) has made itself evident in your life recently?"*

"How silly my desperation for validation is," she responded. *"It will never be enough, and it is already more than enough. This is an ongoing battle for me. Perhaps one of the fundamental reasons I do what I do (please applaud for me, please applaud for me!). It's one of the reasons I think I need to step away or at least shift my approach to my career.*

... And a feeling of home. I think I still spend a good portion of my time seeking that feeling. A lot of homesickness in my life and I'm not totally sure what that means other than a yearning for acceptance and a physical ache in my belly."

"I imagine that this triggers imposter syndrome for you, as it definitely does in me," I said. *"The more I do or give back, the harder it is for me to feel good about it. It is such a struggle point in my own life, yet I know I am adding value to others, just as you are. So, that was a long way to say, **please** don't step fully away from your work as it is impacting the lives of others (mine too) in a very positive way. And I also fully understand your sentiments. The paradox of life is alive and kicking!"*

She gave me a crooked smile and said, *"I've been in a crazy contemplative mood since last weekend. I had the opportunity to meet David Copperfield. I was selected out of the audience to participate as part of his show and had a meet and greet with him after. It wasn't so much a meet and greet as he comes up and takes a pic with you and then runs away. The whole experience made me so deeply sad.*

Here's a man who is worth a billion, easy. He owns a half dozen islands in the Caribbean. He's married to a model. He's quite literally magical. From the outside, it looks like he has it all. But there is something so profoundly sad about his persona. So achingly lonely. I think he only knows how to do, not to be. Who is David Copperfield if he isn't doing two shows a day in Vegas?

I don't ever want to be that!"

With raised eyebrows and a gentle shaking of my head in disbelief, my response flowed out as, *"What an experience to meet Copperfield and witness what you did. It's all a facade, isn't it? With almost everyone. Virtually no one lives in integrity and integrity starts with ourselves. Loving ourselves. Trusting ourselves. It's such a foreign concept to most people, including me for most of my life.*

A life partner, money, things, whatever, can never ever make you happy or fill the void. You're either complete with what's inside or you're not. Everything else leads to expectation hangovers. He's definitely learned (still learning?) that the hard way."

It should come as no surprise that the concept of inner trust is generally rejected by science. Jonas Nordstrom told me, "*Where psychology goes wrong sometimes is when it takes the positivistic model of science, where they say you shouldn't base your understanding on your own experience. Instead, they base their understanding of psychology on research articles, which can be far away from the truth. Because, in 100 years, the understanding of psychology through research articles will be so much further ahead of where we are today, due to it being such a new science.*

When a therapist in Sweden, for instance, doesn't relate what they read to their own experience, it becomes difficult to be able to distinguish that, 'This is my own experience, so it doesn't matter whether it's true or not, but I can relate to what I am reading in this scientific article and determine if it is true to me, and how, and when is it not true.' This is when we start navigating all of the variables.

American psychotherapists are more prone to trust their own experience, and relate what they're learning to that, because they're not afraid of what other people think. A little simplified, but in the Swedish village mentality, they're programmed not to trust what they experience and believe but instead rely more on what they read."

Integrity is an ongoing process of allowing our inner and outer experiences to complement each other, despite our very human flaws. It all starts with a deep inner trust.

A trust this deep takes time. It takes exploration. In her book, *The Top Five Regrets of the Dying*, Bronnie Ware writes that the most common regret of her hospice patients was *"I wish I'd had the courage to live a life true to myself, not the life others expected of me."*

It takes dedication to ourselves to live this way. At times, especially in the beginning stages when we are first getting comfortable with ourselves and our power, feelings of vanity and selfishness can creep in. The outside world projects all types of "shoulds" and "shouldn'ts" on us.

Don't let them in!

They are not for us. They are nothing more than other people's fears and lack of their own inner trust. As we are able to trust ourselves and align our living with our true North, self-esteem skyrockets.

None of this guarantees that we can or will live in integrity. Living from a state of integrity across all aspects of our life is intense. It's not comfortable nor does it feel natural, until there becomes no other option.

Only deep self-love can bring about the security needed to fully lean into inner trust, leading to a life lived in full integrity. The recipe here calls for nothing other than inner trust and self-love. No substitutions, please.

I just snorted as I thought about this in my own life. I lived in la-la land for so many years and then, taking a huge risk, or so it felt like at the time, stepped one foot onto the path of integrity, wholeheartedly believing that I was finally all in. Feelings of joy washed over me. I was elated. At peace. A smile settled into the creases of my face.

Then life happened. To me, as me, and all around me. My evenings would be spent questioning why it wasn't easier, what all of it meant, and trying to figure out how to reset things for the next day. Sleepless nights followed and migraines crept back into my life. Why had I taken the risk to step into integrity, just to bring more hurt and frustration into my life?

The first sign of the delusion I was telling myself came after waking up in a pool of sweat one morning. It was the third night in a row where I had been secretly listening to the inner voice at night yet denying it day after day. This was definitely *not* living in inner integrity. Using this as a jumping-off point for a deeper dive into what the heck was actually going on, I found that I didn't actually have both feet on the path.

Huh. This whole time I thought I was all in, and I wasn't even close. The pain and suffering I endured were so intense because I was hobbling along, one foot on the path and one in the weeds. The fact that I was limited in speed, agility, and capability was lost on me. Having to constantly adapt in order to survive yet being blind to it all. Being out of congruency made things unnecessarily hard and intensely painful. I needed to get both feet on the path.

Integrity is a path, not a destination, and it's only relevant in the present moment.

--- -- - *Just Show Up* - -- ---

"Q: How can I live in the Now?
A: You already do. You just haven't noticed."

- **Byron Katie,** *Loving What Is*

We spend a lot of time in our society talking about and setting goals. Planning, preparing, tracking, implementing, and all the other systems we build around successfully achieving our goals. Why? Plain and simple, because they work.

Goals are good. Yay goals!

Goals are also some of the most frustrating things we have to contend with in our daily lives. I don't know about you, but I stopped setting New Year's resolutions (just another type of goal), as 99% of the time they fell apart and I felt like a failure.

Why does this dichotomy exist? On one hand we know that goals work, yet on the other, we have countless examples of where and when they don't. The graveyard of unmet goals in my timeline is stacked pretty darn high.

Let's unpack this. For starters, we know that to achieve a desired result, setting and having goals provides intentionality, which is not all that bad. In fact, it's a great start. As we've already discussed in chapter 4, creating intentionality drastically increases the odds of you achieving a desired result, and setting a goal is the act of being intentional. We also learned that stopping here, and not adding in intent, means that the added benefit is weakened, and its efficacy can be reduced by half.

The real problem with how we set goals is when we subscribe to silly acronyms like S.M.A.R.T. goals. This is awesome if you are trying to sell a book or to get more followers on Twitter or TikTok, but for those of us in the trenches trying to get shit done in our lives, this technique is less than helpful. Let me explain. When we use the five components to this technique, we are incorporating **S**pecific, **M**easurable, **A**ttainable, **R**ealistic, and **T**imely components into our goals. On the surface this sounds really good. So good that I personally bought into it and incorporated it into my daily life for over two decades.

The SMART method does work, sometimes. If it didn't occasionally do the job, no one would use it. So, let's be clear, it works. It's just not efficient and can often leave us feeling like losers due to the nature of the built-in rigidity around its structure.

In my experience, I achieve about 1 out of every 10 SMART goals that I set. That's a 10% win rate over the 20 years that I've used this method. Ouch! The reason, I believe, can be explained by analyzing it with the Fuck-It filter.

FOCUS - is it internal or external?
UNCONDITIONAL - are we judging ourselves every step along the way?
CHANGE - is it allowed and appreciated?
KEEP - is the #1 rule to keep showing up while embracing change?
INTENT - is this precursor (intent) to intentionality playing an active role?
TRUE - are you able to stay in integrity with yourself?

FOCUS. Focus is the first place where things typically go sideways, and it usually starts at the beginning when we first set a goal. We look outside ourselves when we start thinking about the specifics, how to measure it, etc. Clearly, we need to be cognizant of external factors and pressures, but we can't control most of these. When we set a goal with an external focus, we are setting ourselves up for failure from day one. When we flip things to an internal focus, it puts us back in the driver's seat.

UNCONDITIONAL. Conditionality is woven into the undertow of our culture. A flavorless soup of if-then judgments forms the base to what we build on top of. Layer by layer there are ones and zeros, ons and offs, yeses and noes that gate our every step. It's like a sea of landmines, which is incredibly difficult to navigate, let alone enjoy the ride along the way.

CHANGE. Change is *not* something we naturally enjoy or appreciate as humans. Not without effort. That's because change takes effort. Effort means paying attention, thinking, iterating, and collaborating. I know, it's a lot. Your reticular activating system (if you don't know by now, Google it) hates me right now. Tough! The rules, the players, and everything involved in this game we call life are constantly changing. We need our goals to be like taffy on a hot summer's day. Gooey and pliable, bending in every direction while leaving a sweet taste in our mouths and a smile on our faces. Leaving us to wonder what flavor we might be lucky enough to get tomorrow.

KEEP. Keep on keeping on! Showing up, day in and day – out, is the easiest and most difficult thing we have to do. In general, SMART goals don't require consistency in this way. If you hit the measurement metric for the day, you can check out. Give up. Be done. That sounds pretty lazy to me. What happens on the days you don't hit the metric? Do you hate on yourself? Tell yourself you suck? That sounds healthy! The reality is that you might crush it one day and totally suck the next. It doesn't matter. Just keep showing up and keep doing your best.

INTENT. Intent is so rarely thought about or executed well. It's the elusive magic sauce we all desperately desire to find and get our hands on. Setting a goal is the act of stepping into intentionality. We could probably use those words interchangeably here, goal and intentionality, if we so desired. A goal without proper intent is virtually worthless, though. Intent is how we show up, not whether we do or don't. It's like putting 87-octane gasoline in a race car when it needs jet-grade fuel and a nitrous oxide booster under the dash. Intent is a daily activity, and it's usually missing from the goals we set.

TRUE. This comes with a very personal question. Are you able to chase your goal while living in integrity? Or are you required, maybe guilted (with self-guilt?), into bending and violating your own truth in order to achieve the desired end? There's no judgment from me here, but this is a slippery slope. Proceed with caution!

When we say, does it pass the Fuck-It filter, what we are saying is, that in order to achieve our greatest desires, and all the small ones too, our goals need the following four ingredients:
- Living, engaging, and acting without constant worry looming over us
- An absence of expectations or self-imposed limitations

- The ability to lean in, have fun, and just go with the flow
- Each day, even though it fluctuates, your best effort is *always* enough

My guess is that as you start to play with running your current goals through this filter, you will find sticky spots. Possibly even a gnarled, twisted, hard knot with sharp protuberances on some of them. I certainly hope you have a degree in woodworking with an apprenticeship under your belt.

If I may, please allow me to pollute the acronym-littered literary landscape with a contribution of my own. I propose that as we look to set goals, we do it with the C.A.N. method, because "Yes You CAN" is the type of positive statement that should accompany a future-based desire, such as a goal. It's extra cheesy, by design, but I promise that this technique will not only work better than SMART goals, but it will keep the power of your choice within your grasps at all times. And it won't leave you feeling less than, no matter the outcome.

CLARIFY. Start from a heady place. Get cerebral and analytical. Then pull back and allow yourself to shift into a heart space. Find coherence between your gut and brain, blending logic with intuition. As your goal starts to take shape, this process will help to align your desires with their true North.

AFFIRM. If you followed the Clarify step properly, then it should naturally flow right into affirmation. Our truths become the basis for our beliefs. With a firm belief that the goal is not only possible, but it **will** happen, we can start to visualize it. Close our eyes and see the movie play out. We watch ourselves achieve the goal and feel what it is like in that future moment. We have succeeded and it feels amazing.

NURTURE. This is how we put it into action. Nurturing only takes one thing: showing up! Of course, showing up leads us into other necessary components, though everything tends to flow into its natural progression from here. When we show up and are present, it becomes obvious what's needed, and we can usually see how to provide it. All of this because we were willing to and found excitement in embracing change.

If you didn't catch it, the Affirm step is where intent comes in. When we start each day and re-Affirm our intentions, we are adding intent to the front end of the process, or the day in this case. We simply step into our belief, visualize it, and then feel the emotions of what success or achievement will be. Sixty seconds is all it takes.

I once owned a bonsai tree and kept it on the windowsill of my kitchen. Each morning I would check the moisture of the soil, visually inspect it for bugs or other signs of stress, and make sure it wasn't getting too much sun. Then I would get out my shears and do a snip here and a clip there. Most days I found myself humming, singing, or talking to the tree. Then I would catch myself and smile.

As the seasons changed it became obvious that my tree needed more light, so I had to find a new spot in my house for it. At first everything seemed peachy, but I noticed some curling at the edges of the leaves on one side of the tree. Narrowing it down, I determined that it was the A/C vent blowing on the leaves for a couple of hours each day. That was an easy fix. From there it was nutrients, sunlight, and mostly my singing that occupied my time with that tree. I sure had fun nurturing it for the five years that I owned it.

Back to control. The only thing in our control is us. Haven't we established that already?

Practice setting goals and managing them in a healthier way that lets you stay in control. The "Yes You CAN" technique, or whatever you want to call it, allows you to remain in your power, retaining choice, which is the most important thing you bring to the table each day. Let go of the form of the goal and don't be overly attached to specific outcomes. Most importantly, create goals from a feeling of alignment with them as well as with who you want to be now, during, and after they are achieved, guaranteeing that your integrity remains intact.

The following is an excerpt from a letter I wrote to my oldest daughter, Cydnie, after she got selected to attend the WAC (Western Athletic Conference) Finals for women's swimming during her freshman year in college:

"Stand with pride. With honor. For the work you have put in to get to this place in life. Flexing all of your skills and talents, allowing them to coalesce into your current journey. Finding success in all aspects of your life. Thriving. Winning.

And what makes me the proudest? It's not the results. **It's a commitment to effort.**

Life will not always bring you success. Or wins. Or happiness. It's the effort we put forth to push through these moments that's the most important. With an eye on how to get to the other side, utilizing the strength it takes to show up and put in the work.

Even when we don't feel like it. Especially when we don't feel like it.

It takes effort. AND YOU GIVE AMAZING EFFORT!"

This is what a goal utilizing the "Yes You CAN" approach looks like. If there's one thing, and only one thing, that separates this from all the other methods and techniques is that its sole focus is on effort, or really, showing up.

The rest is just noise.

Show up.
To Life.
Everyday.

--- -- - *Meaningfully Specific* - -- ---

Sometimes I like to pretend that I'm at a cocktail party and I've just run into my ego. He is commandeering my time and is talking my ear off. And while I appreciate his friendship, I want to mingle, say hi to my other friends, and meet some new people. Instead of getting angry and telling him off, I choose to show some compassion. I grab his hand, look him in the eye, and thank him for his friendship. I'm also honest with him that I am at this event to visit with other people, in addition to him. With that, I hug him and let him know that I'll make sure to find him to say goodbye before I leave. I turn to my left and casually walk away.

There are many ways to honor who the ego is, express gratitude for him, and also set firm boundaries. The ego deserves to be treated like anyone else in your life in a way that says, "*You matter to me*," yet implicitly expresses that he isn't the *only* thing that matters to you.

This is balance.
Available to us through awareness.

Awareness allows us to witness our thoughts, feelings, and emotions without the need to condemn or eradicate them. To be human and have human reactions, yet not be moved to action by them. If we do choose to act, we can act *with* instead of acting because of. An example here is fear. Odds are you will never completely eradicate fear from your life. When it does show up, step into your power of choice. You can choose to acknowledge that the fear exists and take action with that understanding instead of the action being driven because of fear.

Gratitude + Honor + Firm Boundaries + Balance + Awareness =

Meaningfully Specific

When we live a life where we extend gratitude, honor those around us, respect our boundaries, and create balance along with an eyes wide open level of awareness, we create a container that changes how we show up to make choices. It's not dissimilar to the premise around the intent to be intentional. Both of these efforts require readiness. Some pregame preparation. Like when we think we can show up to a tennis match against Roger Federer yet haven't swung a racket since 8th grade.

My good friend German's (the same guy from chapter 6) dad is the type of person who always makes the wrong choice. If there's a bottle of Coke and a bottle of water in front of him, he'll go for the Coke bottle. Because, for him, he believes water is healthier, and therefore, a more difficult choice. It could also be that he is blind to the choice in front of him and sees the bottle of Coke sitting alone on the table. Yet he fails to see that he had a choice in what he allowed himself to see. The choice before the choice.

Sadly, this has led him into a deep depressive cycle. One where he can't look himself in the mirror because he has been unable to make even one good decision in his life. This weighs heavily on German, who I had recently bumped into at a coffee shop where the subject of his dad came up as his health had been deteriorating lately. The following was our conversation:

Brent: *I believe that the reason you have the story you do, can talk like you talk, and make analogies like you do is because deep down, you truly love yourself. And when you love yourself, you trust yourself. I'm not saying you don't have work to do. We all do. Your dad, on the other hand, has no love for himself, which means he lacks trust in himself. And that's the reason he can't make any "right" or healthy decisions. It's impossible until we learn to put ourselves first.*

German: *Learning to love yourself. Let's dig into that because it's very interesting. I never thought about this before in the way I'm going to share this thought.*

Learning to love yourself, for me, means that you need to get to the core of what really matters to you. To be able to see in yourself what you would in a third party. Then you have to align "who you are really" with "who you're being." This requires clarity, because you need to hear yourself talk. And a lot of people don't ever give themselves the time to go that deep. To really say, "You know what? You wanted to be a surfer all your life, but you hate the water. You hate the cold. You hate waking up in the morning. That's not you at all. So, let that go.

It hits you that you're only setting yourself up to suffer, and it hurts because you realize that these idols that you've had since you were a kid (cowboys, surfers, astronauts, nurses) start disappearing from your life. Instead, you find that you're really just a bookworm. That every time you spend the day in a cozy chair at home reading a book, there's a spark. A thrill. Finding and owning this alignment can be so powerful. It also dawns on you that you can't fully love yourself without accepting this new you. Are you cool with that? Are you cool with what you found out? Because learning to love yourself is a dual thing. It's learning what you need and executing it. It is not just learning to be aware of the need to love yourself. You are the person who loves and the one that does the action that promotes the love unto yourself.

Brent: *I love to watch your eyes as you think through this stuff. It's a privilege to watch you connect with your soul. My personal experience is a little different, yet it's all the same. One of the big things I had to come to grips with and then let go of is what I thought defined me. You were speaking of having to let go of the dream of being a surfer one day, and, as I've held the title of CEO for the last ten years, I am now no longer one. It no longer defines me. It's part of my journey and my story but it's not a piece of me. It never was. It was just a temporary overlay, like a jacket. Ha, a "Members Only" jacket!*

If somebody asks today what I've learned in terms of loving myself, I can honestly say that I'm just Brent. My career of running businesses, stepping into this author role, playing sports, heading up leadership groups, traveling around the world...none of that is me. I did or do them all, yet they don't define me. I don't need them to make me feel better about myself or make me feel accomplished.

German: *That's interesting because when people ask me, what do you do? There's always a certain conflict inside of me. I own a company, I wear 30 hats, and yet my passion is as a designer and a creator. So, for me, this does define me because I do live life through the creation of things.*

Brent: *Let me challenge you on this. You have become very good at tapping into your creative energy and what comes out of you from this place is special. It's beautiful. If it went away tomorrow and all that was left was just you, nothing changes. The love I have for you. The love your wife has for you. Nothing changes who you are.*

German: *I can stop doing graphic design or I can stop owning a company or I can...but I cannot stop creating.*

Brent: *This is true. We are all creators. It is our choices that create our lives. I know that you've felt an attachment to being a creator at a level that's different from other people, and you are an amazing creator who has been able to tap into this energy and use it to enhance other areas of life. If that were to go away, you would still be the creator of your life.*

German: *Yes, yes, that I totally agree with. It's hard sometimes, but I know it to be true at my core.*

Brent: This is what makes you a beautiful human. Not because you've applied it to ways that are successful and interesting as a graphic designer. I also have applied my creativity to the entrepreneurial side of running businesses. Even though I am not applying it in that way anymore, I'm taking that same creative energy and channeling it into other places.

All we have is our ability to create. Creating is what we were designed to do.

German: And it's interesting because you're creating things even when you're not creating anything. Your energy is splashing on the world around you, at home and everywhere. On that day you decide to relax and stay on the couch watching movies with your kids, you're creating bonds. You're creating cuddles or connectivity at that level. There's always the creation of something, right?

Brent: Absolutely. This is where the fun choices come down to. We could look at that same situation and you could be four beers or a bottle of wine deep. You could be completely numbed out and not present, choosing to create a different story, or choosing not to choose. Versus the alternative narrative, where you say, I get to sit on this couch, let go of everything else, and just cuddle. These are the little choices that start to stack. They build on each other over time. These are the spaces in between, and they are more meaningful than we typically give them credit for.

Let me give you an example of what, at least for me, feels very relevant. Last night my daughter and I got back from her high school basketball game at 8:45 pm. She was starving, so we quickly made dinner. Okay, let's be real, I made dinner. By the time we were done, it was 9:20 pm. She went upstairs to finish homework and get ready for bed, as we had to wake up at 5:45 am. I hung back in the kitchen getting ready for the next day, cleaning things up and making her lunch. I finally sat down at 9:40, the first time all day. I sent her a text saying that I was going to decompress and sit on the couch and watch part of my TV show for 20 minutes. It was my attempt to say, "Please give me some quiet time." I was on the couch for maybe four minutes and she called me, because that's what you do when you're a teenager. Apparently, their legs stop working after 8 pm. I picked up the phone and asked her, "What's up?" She said, "Can you come rub my back?" Part of me wanted to say, "No, I need my downtime. I need to decompress. I deserve to have some peace and quiet. I even took the time to communicate that via text. On top of that, I just spent 40 minutes making dinner and cleaning it all up."

There's always a choice looming in the background somewhere. I paused, allowed myself to become aware of this, and chose to look at it as, wow, my daughter just wants me to be present with her. And while this choice may seem easy to you, it hasn't been for me in the past. My selfish thoughts were, "I've already given hours upon hours of my time tonight." But it is a choice in the moment where life hands you an opportunity and I see them as beautiful now. Even so, there's still a part of me, my first reaction, where I think, "I have to get up from the couch?" And after taking a second to get present and coherent, I tell myself, "Of course, you're going to get up from the couch, give her a ten-minute back rub, and spend the time connecting with your daughter." My heart fills with gratitude as I realize what a privilege, a special gift, this time to connect really is.

German: *I wonder how many of those types of choices do we not step into the power of? And where else do they show up? I would guess that they aren't always this obvious, and I would argue that they're all over the place.*

As Tony Robbins has said, *"In your head, you're dead. In your heart, you're smart."* Living a life where we show up as meaningfully specific is when life starts to open up for us. Showing itself, exposing the inner beauty, and allowing the fragile scent to be received in all its glory by our olfactory glands. A circular flow of signals tickles our senses, reminding us that this present moment is the human experience.

In-joy!

PAPERCUTS

Chapter 8:
FLUENCY

--- -- - *Authentically Real* - -- ---

One of my all-time favorite bands is Depeche Mode. They are one of about five bands that made it out of the '80s alive and profitable. In 2023, their 42nd year as a band, they were still selling out stadiums all over the world. The Rock and Roll Hall of Fame inducted them in 2020 and they hold the 98th spot on VH1's greatest artists of all time. And yet, many Americans don't know who they are or, if they do, not much more about them than their name.

Being able to sell out 30,000 seat venues in a matter of minutes, speaks to their cult-like following. During their 5th decade touring, nonetheless. So, what's their secret?

I think it boils down to two things. They have never sold out. Musically speaking, they have remained true to the soul of what made them unique from the start. Of course, it has evolved over time, but it always pays homage to where they came from. The other rarity among bands is that they are insane performers. They bring it and leave everything out on the stage, every night. A truly exemplary model of what it looks like to show up.

In short, they are the real deal rock stars.

My friend Thomas, a Swede living in Spain, sent me a text asking if I'd listened to their album that dropped in March of 2023. It had been seven years since the previous one, so there was some pent-up excitement leading up to the release. I hadn't heard about it yet, so I quickly cleared my schedule to spend the next 50 minutes and 25 seconds letting their sound consume me.

Honestly, I was disappointed. What can I say? I wasn't impressed. It was mid-afternoon for me in Phoenix and 11 pm in Benidorm, Spain, but I didn't care. *"What is this shite?"* I punched into our WhatsApp chat. I was annoyed and disappointed. Seven years and this is what I waited for?

Three dots appeared, meaning he was still up and willing to entertain my sarcastic petulance.

"Normally, with Depeche Mode, I need to 'listen in'," he typed. There was a cool and calm nature to his response. *"Seldom it just clicks direct. Those songs are normally sticky for a long time, vs. catchy—things that sound great initially and then fade quickly."*

I froze, my heart thumping faster now. Looking up and to the right, I found myself shaking my head as my eyes rolled backward. Of course. He was so right! It's one of the biggest reasons this band has such a devoted fan base. The fleeting whims of the average teenager don't connect with their music. The expression of their art takes patience and time to unfold and speak to the listener through a combination of lyrics, sounds, and on-stage delivery.

My body flushed and I wondered, how often do we take the time to "listen in" in our lives?

As I reflect on my own journey, my life is speckled with quick decisions on half-baked information, drowned in a syrup of assumptions, expectations, and biased overlays. While I couldn't see it at the time, it's painfully obvious to me now that most people never stood a chance when interacting with me. I rarely, if ever, took the time or was present enough to hear and feel their truth.

Jumping from wave top to wave top, I resisted the urge to surf into the troughs. What if I got stuck and then the next wave swallowed me? What if I could never recover? My fear prevented me from taking a bold step into curiosity. I kept telling myself, *"It's safer on the surface. You're simply being smart and protecting yourself."*

The practice of floating on the surface wasn't just an outward habit. I turned it inward too. The stories and lies I could weave for myself were obnoxiously complex and riddled with guilt. A cocoon of shame was slowly being knit around me, bringing warmth and comfort to the delusion I was painting. Paralysis soon followed. One wrong move and the lies would unravel what I had so eloquently built.

Eventually, I found myself out of moves. Checkmate!

Authenticity and being real were concepts long out of reach.

The Gospel of Thomas teaches us that, "*If you bring forth what is within you, what you bring forth will save you. If you do not bring forth what is within you, what you do not bring forth will destroy you.*"

As we've been learning on this journey together, all is not lost. We are awake now! We have awareness. It's never too late to find a new wellspring of energy that is instantly available to us. With it, we wield our choice with confidence while tapping into our inner power. The path diverges and our journey presents us with the opportunity to break through the cocoon of the ego and let our inner butterfly out.

No longer bound by the chain of lies or the web of fear, we start to listen in on ourselves. It's ugly at first. Full of bumps, gotchas, and scary what-if ghosts hiding in the shadows. The deeper we go, the more we must push forward and move through it. A faint light reflects off the edges, illuminating the cracks and crevices. The shadows grow smaller and begin to dissipate from the ever-increasing brightness that is all around us now.

Blinking our eyes, allowing dilation to bring things back into focus, everything is out in the open and completely visible. All the pain. All the stories. All the lies. There's nothing to hide behind as the light is implicitly penetrating.

Integrity, inside and out.
It's empowering, isn't it?
Freeing. Natural. A state of homeostasis.
With no bags in tow. Nothing lingering.
Breathe that in.
That's presence. In the present.
The possibility of connection.
Down in the troughs.
Humans being humans.
Living at depth. Owning our truth.
Life is beautiful!
Simple. Peaceful. Without worry.
The freedom to stop doing,
The permission to start being.

Getting here isn't easy, but once you find your way, it's sticky. Grounding. You won't want to leave. There is no other way to live life. A life lived out in the open is ineffably freeing. So light, airy, and carefree. This is what it feels like to be. No more doing, just being.

Life tastes and smells different from this vantage point. What once would have sucked you in like a siren calling to a salt-crusted sailor, the world's seductive powers are exposed for what they really are: false prophets peddling lies. Now, these deceptions are no longer passing our newly developed Fuck-it filter.

The following passage from *The Kin of Ata Are Waiting for You*, by Dorothy Bryant, sums it up perfectly:

"The world is full of ways to try and reach it. Drugs and drink and sex and fame and things ... plenty of things. You can spend years, from your first shiny tricycle to your last taste of power, and take a long, long time before you know finally, fully, before you realize that you always come down, no matter how high you've been; that it's a law of gravity of the soul."

When we live in integrity, authenticity finds us. The two cannot live without each other, like two lovers who have found themselves entangled through the millennia.

David Richo reminds us, "*I cherish my own integrity and do not use it as a yardstick for anyone else's behavior.*" Integrity, with authenticity in tow, is in reference to our truth. The truth that we find deep inside our souls. A truth that is only for us. Individually, uniquely, and sustainably for us alone.

Being real and living in integrity is how we honor ourselves at the highest level. Expressing a deep love for ourselves. One that says, **"I trust you," even when it feels like the world doesn't.** Once this stage is set, something interesting begins to happen. Beauty and serendipity show up in the most unexpected and delightful of ways.

Just as the petal of a flower falls open to allow the light in, life begins to reveal itself.

--- -- - *Hide & Seek* - -- ---

Turning over rocks, looking behind walls, stepping through doorways, and staring out the window of an airplane. These are but a few of the ways we go about discovering life. Reading books, engaging in conversations, looking in the mirror, and feeling our *feels* provide us with a more focused lens, pointed at ourselves. Discovery is baked into all facets of our daily lives.

Getting lost in this process is so easy that, at times, it can feel like it's almost a rite of passage. When our journey becomes all-consuming with having to know, to discover, what is. What and who we are. What the world is and is not. The never-ending rabbit hole of historical events and places, viewpoints, perspectives, recollections, interpretations, ancient stories, cultural myths, fairy tales, and yesterday's dinner.

Did you happen to catch what all of these discoveries have in common?

They are echoes of the past.
Ghosts.
Gone and never to return.

When we grasp this, it's immediately obvious what the "secret to life" is not. It is definitely <u>not</u> about discovering the past.

What, then, is the deeper meaning? What is it that is right under our nose and yet we somehow can't see it? Seemingly out of focus, we are unable to put our finger directly on it. Life has us caught in a game of hide and seek with no apparent winners. Beauty, excitement, pain, love, disgust, and happiness all happen at once, then are lost and hidden in the past.

Why are we so desperately seeking to understand and uncover the past?

Neale Donald Walsch proselytizes, *"The deepest secret is that life is not a process of discovery, but a process of creation. You are not discovering yourself but creating yourself anew. Seek, therefore, not to find out Who You Are, seek to determine Who You Want to Be."*

As we begin to show up and step into the present moment, we discover who we are at that exact second. Then it's gone. We aren't "that" anymore. We are something slightly different. It's constantly changing. Morphing. Fleeting.

It's not that discovery isn't available to us or damn interesting at times. The challenge comes when we live and act only from a place of discovery. This is how we get lost in the shadows, struggling to find our way back to the light. To the present.

I don't know about you, but this feels incredibly heavy. How in the heck are we supposed to know who we want to be?

According to Jonas Nordstrom, *"We can start to build a relationship with our inner teacher, once we find him/her, and have them lead us on the journey, if we allow it. People and experiences are curated for us. We just need to ask the right questions to find the lessons in virtually every aspect of life."*

This is where our long-held belief systems can become sticking points and speed bumps in our journey. The backbone to our beliefs can potentially become destabilized, which can be terrifying. At the same time, the only way to build something bigger, better, and more solid is to strip away the past, demolishing the old layers.

In life, this looks like showing up to the present in surrender.

Similarities to restoring an old car are worthy of comparison. One must first remove the doors, take the seats and engine out, and slowly work toward stripping everything out of the car. Then the frame gets sandblasted, all the rust is removed, and it gets a fresh coat of paint. Now that we have a solid foundation, the rest of the car can be cleaned, polished, and put back together. This results in something that is not only more beautiful but much more functional and built to last another 50 years.

Jonas went on to add, "*So many people don't think they need to learn or grow. Yet this is where fear comes in. This is also where they might have enough awareness to reach out and ask for the opinion of someone like me, yet I know that they don't really want to hear what I have to say.*

It's at this point where we have to stop and ask ourselves a very serious question, 'Do we really want to learn, to grow, and to find out who we want to become? Or is it easier and more comfortable to have confirmation of our current reality and the way things currently are for us?'

I've found that most people don't even realize that they do not want to step into the present. They just know that getting confirmation of their current reality is safer and feels less scary on the surface. The depth of our fears begins to get exposed as well as our fight and flight triggers."

Let's be honest, this is not easy work because the easy route, the one filled with complacency, is also full of addictions. It's like trying to cut sugar out of your diet completely. It's healthy for you, will help you live longer, and might even get you those six-pack abs you've always dreamt about, but it requires giving up those fun-filled dopamine hits. Choices!

This is the moment when we discover that our intellect is a sneaky little bugger. Mine can be a total asshole. At least that's how he shows up on the regular. Of course, what we're really talking about here again is the ego. Our ego relishes the past, is fearful of the future, and hates public speaking, I mean, being present. God forbid he shows up ready to see what the world has for him today. Nope! He's donning head-to-toe chain mail and ducking behind a fifty-pound shield. Sorry, present moment, you are not going to get him!

In my own journey, I got so frustrated that at one point I nicknamed my ego a not so nice curse word that rhymes with Muck Mace. We did not get along for a long time and I would call him out, by name, shaming and berating him each time he got in my way. Then I realized that I had been stooping to his proverbial level. Pile on the papercuts!

It wasn't until I looked my ego in the eye, gave him a hug, and truly understood where he made decisions from that things started to improve for me. The ego isn't hiding in the shadows trying to trip us up constantly. He's there as a protector. A first line of defense with lightning quick reaction speeds.

We can find gratitude for the ego from this place. Knowing that our life on this planet requires the skill set he has to offer. Just not all the time. Think about him like your own personal chef. One that knows you, your likes and dislikes, how often you get hungry, and when you need carbs versus proteins to perform at your best in life. This takes practice to get here though, starting with awareness and firm boundaries. Left to his own devices, he might show up as your Italian aunt who likes to make five pounds of spaghetti with a side of butter-slathered garlic bread and stands over you until you finish your third plate. Out of complete respect, of course.

When appreciated, seen, and trained, your inner chef will make you something healthy, listen to your desires, and (mostly) take care of you when you aren't paying attention. Just watch out that he doesn't bring his knives to bed with you.

Our chef, I mean ego, is stuck in our body yet operates solely from our brain. We are wise to remember just how powerful this voice is, especially in the moment, and how easily it can persuade us in or out of almost any decision. We get stuck in the rationale of running choices through our logic loop and forget that we have emotions, feelings, and our "three" brains—gut, heart, and head.

There are many things that our minds just can't know, yet our bodies intuitively do. It's imperative that we get comfortable with the fact that it is not always possible to explain or rationalize our gut feelings. Our ego will need to honor the boundaries we put in place and start to trust us in return. If that's not possible, we can put our ego in "time out." Be forewarned that he will kick and scream if you do this.

Back to the present, to us. Especially when we feel stuck, there is great value in relaxing into, listening to, and trusting our intuition. Allowing for the realization to sink in that we *can* be in control, even when the ego tells us we can't. The power that lies within our gift of choice is energizing and exotic in the potential it holds.

When stuck in my head,
I come back to the present.
Focus on the five senses,
The symphony of sensations they create,
All of them are inputting at the same time.
It's exhilarating. Unique. Beautiful.
Overwhelming in the most perfect way.
This is what it means to be human.
It's the portal to connection, with self and others.
Surrendering, ultimately, to this moment.
Achieving presence, through being,
Leading to momentous joy.

These are the moments when we can perceive peace, taste love and breathe life in through big smiles. A concoction for happiness that dances among us like the exhale from the Cheshire Cat's hookah. Floating, twisting, and weaving all around while slowly dissipating. The moment is gone, but there are infinitely more of them available to us.

We can create more moments like this by taking action. Action from choice. And as Jay Papasan and Gary Keller emphasize in their book, *The One Thing*, "*In life, every action you take is a vote for the type of person you want to be.*"

I would take this a step further and say that every action we take is a brushstroke on the painting of the life we desire to create for ourselves.

--- -- - *Chasing Happy* - -- ---

"Total abandon is the junction at which freedom and awe collide."

- **Me**

How often do we find ourselves caught in the inner narrative of, *"I'll be happy when…?"* We design a plan governed by expectations and rules about how, at some random point in the future, if the stars align, then, and only maybe then, will we be happy.

This happened last December when a friend of mine called and said, *"I'm currently planning a big year in which I'm chasing awe. I know, I know, I don't like the idea of chasing either, but I haven't found the right word yet to describe my plan."*

"Hmmm," was my reply. *"Are you sure you're not chasing confirmation? I think you might just find what you're looking for in the mirror. That there really isn't anything to chase because you already have it. You already **know** it. Being open to seeing the awe in others, in the world, and in everything around us is simply a shift in perspective. One that I am chasing at the moment. Or manifesting. Or allowing to show up!"*

"This is exactly it," she said, her voice pinging with excitement. *"It's funny, but knowing this doesn't seem to help. I'm working on patience, which is the key for me. You can't try. You can't force. You just have to be and allow what will be to be as well—and that seems to be a real challenge for me. Stillness. Patience. Letting go."*

"Letting go," I said, nodding my head. *"This has been a major theme for me in the last year too. Funny enough, I am starting to see that letting go is the key to creating. I too am plagued with knowing yet struggling to integrate the lessons in my daily life. Why is it so hard?"*

She closed her eyes and breathed out her nose, in the aha! kind of way, and said, *"I guess because it wouldn't be worth it otherwise? Or maybe that's just the bullshit lines we feed ourselves. I don't know, but I'm just trying to let go. More and more it's letting go rather than forcing that seems to be working for me."*

That's when it hit me that Henry David Thoreau already captured this so eloquently when he said, *"Happiness is like a butterfly: the more you chase it, the more it will evade you, but if you notice the other things around you, it will gently come and sit on your shoulder."*

My therapist and friend, Diana, has been a huge support in my life. She regularly provides me with wise counsel, the space to break things from time to time and gently applies salve to my many, many papercuts. We had been discussing this book and she wrote me the following after letting our conversation marinate a bit:

"Life and every moment in it is a gift. If we don't open these gifts with intent, we can enjoy the package but not really experience the essence of what's inside. As we go deeper, we are reminded that every moment is a choice. When we can approach our life with the consciousness that comes from intentionality, we deepen our experience many times over.

And isn't that what life is about...to be fully present, every moment, with every experience? Not just the temporary pleasures of life, but the 'all' of life?"

This is a beautiful reminder that happiness cannot be found. It is not something we can chase or pursue. Neither can someone else provide it for us.

As we learn to live a life built on the framework of being purposely intentional, a funny thing happens. The opposite shows up. As we shift our focus internally and live a life of integrity based on our truths, we can finally begin to let go of any control we thought we had outside of ourselves. Stepping out of that delusion and feet first into leading with compassion and unconditional love, it becomes impossible not to step in puddles of great joy.

This leads to an existence of total abandon. Allowing the world to show up and happen through us. As us. The collision point of freedom and awe. These are the moments when we experience happiness. It lands on our shoulders and whispers in our ears. Stimulating a glowing smile that leaves us with a satiety of peace.

As it flutters off, we are left knowing that life is beckoning us to stop chasing. To stop "doing." It's our drive for doing that has caused all of the papercuts we have had to endure.

The deepest desire of life itself is that we start being. That we conspire to live life with total abandon! Showing up, in surrender, and letting life happen for us.

Fortuitously, all it takes is the one thing we have each been gifted. CHOICE!

PAPERCUTS

Chapter 9:
AFTERWORD

--- -- - *Self-Care-Ish* - -- ---

It's time to start showing up for ourselves. What is often seen as selfish at first glance is really just self-care. As the old adage goes, you can't give what you don't have.

The first step to being able to take hold of and exercise choice at any given point in time is to take control of our inner reactions to external and internal events. This allows us to see through the fog, the constant distractions, and blaring noises.

- Practice mindfulness and self-awareness by observing thoughts and feelings *without* judgment. Observe and acknowledge without ignoring or shoving them down.

- Learn to distinguish between what can and cannot be changed, focusing on what we can change.

- Go into nature (or your side yard). Daily. Alternate between sweating (moving) and sitting still. Soak it all in. The sounds. The smells. The texture of the terrain on the soles of your feet. Learn to observe, understand and respect nature, and start to align your life with it.

- Cultivate the virtues of wisdom, courage, and self-control, all while fiercely practicing kindness, compassion, and empathy toward yourself and others.

- Find a path to living in integrity. There is nothing that will better build the foundation for a long-lasting and healthy life. One that allows us to step into our agency of choice, at all moments, as a life of integrity will. I would even go so far as to say that self-love and trust aren't possible and definitely not sustainable without living a life of integrity, at all costs.

For more tips on unspinning the web each of us has built, finding a path to integrity and other healthy rituals, visit: www.3xBold.com

PAPERCUTS

Chapter 10:
ACKNOWLEDGEMENTS

There are so many people that I would like to honor for their contributions to this book and to my life. Some were actively and knowingly giving, while others had no idea about their generous offerings. It matters not how the gifts each of them have given me arrived in my life, as I receive them all with honor and gratitude.

Mom – for the love you gave, the love you withheld and passion you brought to being the most devoted grandma ever. Dad – for all the evenings sitting in the spa, learning Spanish, practicing swearing and telling jokes. Troy – for always being there. Always being willing to help or listen. You are what everyone would want in a brother. Britt – for two decades of friendship, experiences, and two amazing daughters. Life wouldn't be the same without our time on earth together. Tamie – for the warm welcome and thoughtfulness that goes into all you do. The self-sacrificing and care for those around you and for hosting Camp Tamie each summer for the grandkids. Jerry – for teaching me about the greatest musicians of our time and all the late-night conversations. And for teaching my kids how to properly put on a fireworks show!

To my daughters, Cydnie and Paisy – I love you both more than you will ever know. My greatest lessons have been learned through you and with you. While unfair, painful and not something I care to repeat, I promise to show up with all the awareness in my power, each and every moment we get together on this journey. You have my deepest apologies but not my regret. It is the stumbling, the falling down and getting back up, that teaches us all – me especially. For that, I honor you both and offer you my unconditional love.

For all the friends I can't even begin to list here. Thank you all for being a part of my life, supporting my journey and helping me paint life with vivid colors. It's been our connection, interaction and shenanigans that have taught me so many lessons along the way.

To the group of Front Row Dads and other friends that stepped in and, though all are novices, did the most professional job of helping me through a developmental edit. Each of your input and contribution has helped to shape this book and has made it more approachable, meaningful and filled with love.

And finally, to everyone that has been a part of my life, thank you. I have no regrets, wouldn't change anything and fully receive the experiences we have had together–from shitty to beautiful.

With humble gratitude.

PAPERCUTS

I spent the first half of life building a career around achievement, reaching C-Suite status, traveling the world, speaking, launching new technologies, and building businesses. After a 7-year journey that led through some dark places, plant medicine ceremonies, and eye-opening realizations, it became evident that nothing external was ever going to fill the void. As the reality of divorce after 18 years of marriage sunk in, I began to see the grind for what it truly was, bringing clarity to what really matters in life. Beginning with a divine 'tap on the shoulder', I stepped out of corporate America, put everything else on hold, and wrote my first book.

'Papercuts: The Art of Self Delusion,' is my first book and has allowed me to bring my passion for a life well-lived and well-traveled to help others integrate and build healthy rituals around being bold in body, mind, and spirit. My home base is in Phoenix, AZ, I am the father of two amazing teenage daughters and am an active member of Front Row Dads - a mastermind and charitable community that prioritizes a family first, business second mindset.

According to one reader:
"Brent's casual yet intimate style, woven together with storytelling, challenges us to wake up and step into our agency. To own the power of choice we have each been gifted and start showing up to life with a deep sense of presence."

To go deeper or to book Brent to speak, visit: www.3xBold.com

Made in the USA
Middletown, DE
07 January 2024